WILEY NATURE EDITIONS

At the Water's Edge: Nature Study in Lakes, Streams and Ponds, by Alan M. Cvancara

Mountains: A Natural History and Hiking Guide, by Margaret Fuller

The Oceans: A Book of Questions and Answers, by Don Groves

Walking the Wetlands: A Hiker's Guide to Common Plants and Animals of Marshes, Bogs, and Swamps, by Janet Lyons and Sandra Jordan

THE
OCEANS

THE
OCEANS

A BOOK OF
QUESTIONS AND ANSWERS

DON GROVES

Wiley Nature Editions
John Wiley & Sons, Inc.
NEW YORK   CHICHESTER   BRISBANE   TORONTO   SINGAPORE

PUBLISHER: Stephen Kippur
EDITOR: David Sobel
MANAGING EDITOR: Frank Grazioli
COPYEDITING: Margaret Yamashita
DESIGN: Stanley S. Drate/Folio Graphics Company, Inc.

This publication is designed to provide accurate and authoritative information in regard to the subject matter covered. It is sold with the understanding that the publisher is not engaged in rendering legal, or other professional services or advice. If legal, or other expert assistance is required, the services of a competent professional person should be sought. FROM A DECLARATION OF PRINCIPLES JOINTLY ADOPTED BY A COMMITTEE OF THE AMERICAN BAR ASSOCIATION AND A COMMITTEE OF PUBLISHERS.

Library of Congress Cataloging-in-Publication Data

Groves, Donald G.
  The oceans : a book of questions and answers / Don Groves.
  p.   cm.—(Wiley nature editions)
  Bibliography: p.
  Includes index.
  ISBN 0-471-60712-6
  1. Oceanography—Miscellanea.   I. Title.   II. Series.
GC28.G76   1989
551.46—dc19   88-32625
                                                            CIP

Printed in the United States of America

   10   9   8   7   6   5

PREFACE

Facts alone are wanted in life. Plant nothing
else, and root minds of reasoning animals
upon facts. Nothing else will ever be of any
service to them.
Thomas Gradgrind in Charles Dickens's
Hard Times

This book was written for people with a general interest in
the world's oceans. I had in mind students, teachers, business
people, divers, writers, lawyers, and others with a desire to learn
more about this vast domain. The book is not intended for the
professional practitioners of oceanography and ocean engineering. For these people, there are already many books and articles
that address various technical aspects of ocean physics, chemistry, biology, geology, meteorology, and engineering. Conversely,
this book, though slightly technical in a few places, requires no
special qualifications of the reader.

The world ocean is an interconnecting body of saltwater
covering over 70 percent of the earth's surface, or 142 million
square miles—more than twice the surface of Mars or nine times
the surface of the moon this world ocean (singular) is made up

of several oceans and seas. These all constitute the earth's most prominent feature, the designer of its surface, the arbiter of its weather, the border of its nations, and the reservoir containing the greatest number of all the living things on this planet. Indeed, the oceans may be the home to so many creatures because they— and we—are in a sense, minioceans unto ourselves. The oceans seem to be in our blood: Nearly three-quarters of our human body fluids bear a striking biochemical similarity to that of ocean water, which is a highly complex solution of dissolved solids, both organic and inorganic, and gases. Furthermore, both the oceans and human body fluids contain living cells, fats, proteins, hormones, carbohydrates, enzymes, vitamins, and antibiotics. Such a similarity has led many authorities to speculate that our primeval ancestors may have emerged from the ocean's cold, wet, pressurized environment.

But however close as we may be to the oceans biologically, we are closest to it emotionally. And we must admit to a kind of feeling of atavistic "at homeness" when we are in, on, or around it. Whether this sensation is real or caused by subconscious influences is unimportant. What is important is that the presence of the ocean has deeply influenced the way of life, the thinking, and the arts and sciences of all civilizations. As such, it has been the impetus for art, for science, and for great works of engineering.

The oceans draw all kinds of people to its shores. By the mid-1990s, according to the U.S. Census Bureau, as many as three out of four Americans will live within 50 miles of a coastline. And this migration is not confined solely to the people of the United States; nearly half of the world's population now lives near the coast, and this percentage is expected to increase in the near future.

As the global population increases, the fragile shorelines of the world, one of the most complicated natural environments on earth, will be used more and more as sites for urban growth, recreation, national defense, industrialization, and commerce.

Nonetheless, the ocean represents the last frontier on this planet, one that is both challenging and promising. The practical applications of its many promising benefits can be realized only with the continued support of ocean science and engineering for national and international needs. Such support requires some understanding, however, by the general public concerning what the ocean scientists and engineers do; what characteristics and processes drive the oceans' physical, chemical, geological, and biological systems; and how many problems of national and international importance may be solved through the broad scientific knowledge of the oceans and their practical exploitation.

It was these thoughts in mind that motivated me to write this book. To carry out this objective I have used a question-and-answer format throughout the book—in the Introduction as well as in the seven chapters: Chapter 1—The Physical Ocean, Chapter 2—The Chemical Ocean, Chapter 3—The Biological Ocean, Chapter 4—The Geological Ocean, Chapter 5—The Meteorological Ocean; Chapter 6—The Engineer's Ocean, and Chapter 7—The Global Ocean—Past, Present, Future. For those who wish to dig deeper into any of the subjects, there is a bibliography at the end of the book. There is also a short glossary of oceanographic terms.

I have used several responsible sources of information to describe the most current developments in the field, mainly recent scientific and technical reports and publications of U.S. government agencies (such as the Office of Technology Assessment, the U.S. Navy, and the National Oceanic and Atmospheric Administration) and the National Research Council. All these sources of information and inspiration are acknowledged in the text or in the bibliography.

Finally, for the many contributions of my wife, Barbara, only one word is needed: indispensable.

CONTENTS

1 THE PHYSICAL OCEAN 17

2 THE CHEMICAL OCEAN 39

3 THE BIOLOGICAL OCEAN   53

4 THE GEOLOGICAL OCEAN   89

5 THE METEOROLOGICAL OCEAN 113

6 THE ENGINEER'S OCEAN 127

7 THE GLOBAL OCEAN—PAST, PRESENT, AND FUTURE 137

TABLES   155

GLOSSARY   163

BIBLIOGRAPHY   181

INDEX   189

THE
OCEANS

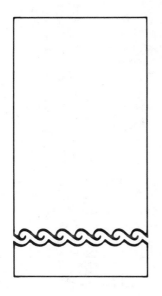

INTRODUCTION

The search for truth is in one way hard and in another easy. For it is evident that no one can master it fully nor miss it wholly. But each adds a little to our knowledge of nature, and from all the facts assembled there arises a certain grandeur.

Aristotle, *Metaphysics*

What are oceanography and ocean engineering?

Oceanography can be defined as the scientific study and exploration of the oceans in all their aspects. It is a large, diversified field of investigation encompassing many sciences: physics, chemistry, biology, geology, and meteorology. Probably, no other area of basic research is as dependent upon the cooperation of different fields of scientific study as is oceanography.

Ocean engineering is also dependent upon interdisciplinary cooperation. Ocean engineers must employ the several branches of established engineering knowledge, together with knowledge of the behavior of the ocean environment, in their applied research endeavors. The work of ocean engineers involves the design, construction, maintenance, and operation of oceanic structures, equipment and devices.

1

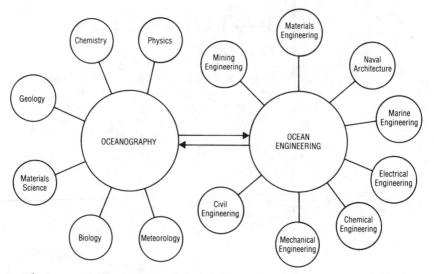

The interactions of oceanography and ocean engineering.

From a practical standpoint, the distinction which is often made between this basic and applied research is sometimes rather misleading since it implies a clear-cut separation that seldom exists in reality. Some research is unquestionably basic, while *applied* research is more concerned with using data from simpler investigations to create working products. The direction of much basic or fundamental research is driven by applied engineering work. In effect, science, whose objectives are to push back the frontiers in understanding the laws of the physical universe, and engineering, the application of science and technology to provide benefits for society, affect one another as complimentary parts of a single process. Each, in the final analysis, is incomplete without the other.

How old is the study of oceanography?

Curiosity about the ocean began in prehistoric times. Ancient peoples, too, were curious about the watery realm that surrounded them. From the time people first stepped into the ocean and swam; fished; dove to bring up pearls, sponges, and shells; and sailed on its surface, they must have become not only interested in it but also forced to learn more about it. As the first "biological oceanographers," they observed the fish and discovered some of the best times and places to find them in quantity. As the first "physical and meterological oceanographers," they witnessed the effects of winds, currents, and tides, and learned either how to use them to advantage or to avoid them. As the first "chemical oceanographers," they found, among other things, that salt could be retrieved from seaweeds and grasses. And as the first "ocean engineers," they learned how to hollow out logs and build rafts for transportation as well as to construct breakwaters and harbors. All these investigations throughout the centuries have been driven by two motivations: to understand the ocean environment and to use this understanding to solve economic and social problems.

Who were some of the early investigators of the ocean?

The earliest investigators of the ocean were fishermen and sailors. Over 2000 years ago the Polynesians used their understanding of the weather, winds, and ocean currents to explore the Pacific. Likewise, early Phoenician and Greek sailors explored the Mediterranean, which the Greeks called Thalassa. To them Thalassa was the body of water that divided the earth into east and west. Beyond this was Oceanus (Okeanos), a huge outer stream that encircled the earth. A few sailors ventured out on Oceanus to unknown distances, some going as far as Iceland, though not knowing that they had ventured beyond the confines of Thalassa.

Although we know almost nothing about these earliest ocean voyages, we do know a bit more about the theories and ideas of some of the early Greeks and Romans. Herodotus (495–428 B.C.), a Greek, believed that the earth was round, and he conducted studies of the Mediterranean Sea that proved helpful to the marine navigators of his time. For example, by comparing depth measurements with samples of the Mediterranean seafloor, he concluded that "the nature of the land of Egypt is such that when a ship is approaching it and is yet one day's sail from shore, if a man try the sounding, he will bring up mud even at a depth of 11 fathoms." (You may have wondered what *fathom* means: It is a nautical term used by sailors to measure depth and thought to be derived from the German word *faden*, meaning "arms out-stretched." When a sailor on a sailing ship measured depth, he would throw forward a weighted line, letting it run through his hands until it touched bottom. Then he would pull up the line and measure out in arm's lengths (approximately six feet) the part that was wet. The fathom is now standardized as equal to six feet).

Another Greek, Aristotle (384–322 B.C.), a pupil of Plato and the tutor of Alexander the Great, described the structure and habits of 180 species of marine animals, and some of his classifications are still considered valid today.

Around 100 B.C., Poseidonius, a Greek geographer, measured 6000-foot depths of the Mediterranean near Sardinia and studied the tides at Cadiz, correlating them with the phases of the moon.

Like Aristotle, the Roman naturalist Pliny (A.D. 23–79) was interested in the forms of life in the ocean. He recognized, just as modern-day scientists do today, that some of these forms could be valuable to humans as sources of medicines. In his treatise *The Natural History*, Pliny discussed possibilities that are only now being realized. Research has shown that many marine organisms and even ocean water itself may contain antibiotics, polysaccharides, steroids, toxins, and other substances helpful in the management of human diseases. To name but a few examples, calcium alginate from one kind of seaweed stops human bleeding; sulfated lamarin from another species of seaweed prevents blood clotting; certain substances isolated from sponges combat viruses and some forms of cancer; and drugs isolated from the sea cucumber and the quahog clam help shrink tumors.

Despite such promising discoveries, however, interest in the ocean waned, as prophesied by the Roman philosopher Seneca (4 B.C.–A.D. 65), who wrote: "An age will come after many years, when the ocean will loose the chains of things, and then also a huge land will lie revealed." This dark age ended in the fifteenth century when attempts to "loose the chains of things" were made by those who applied their knowledge of elementary navigation to explore the oceans of the world and seek "the huge land" that Seneca had said would be revealed. Until this time, the Europeans had concentrated their interest on the Mediterranean. But with the Renaissance, thinkers rediscovered some of the ancient Greek scholars, who had mathematically proved that the world was round. They also reexamined the writing of Ptolemy, the geographer of Alexandria, who, in the second century A.D. had said that circumnavigation of the earth was feasible "except for want of resolution and the scarcity of provision."

What did the explorers of the fifteenth and sixteenth centuries learn about the ocean?

In 1416, Prince Henry of Portugal established a center, Sagres, for the study and dissemination of navigation and other oceanographic information. Sagres, located on the southwestern tip of Portugal, produced many naval architects and explorers. In fact, both Christopher Columbus and Vasco de Gama—who between 1497 and 1499 found a route to India via the Cape of Good Hope—were students at Sagres. Columbus, a skillful navigator who rediscovered America in 1492, also became an oceanographer while on his voyages, which were the culmination of Renaissance, the intellectual, technological, and commercial revolution taking place in Europe at that time. During his four voyages, Columbus collected and studied marine flora and fauna, noted currents and weather, and discovered the Sargasso Sea (an area in the North Atlantic where the so-called Sargasso weed collects in large quantities). Between 1519 and 1521, the Portuguese navigator Ferdinand Magellan sailed to the Pacific Ocean, where he measured some of its depths. On one occasion he measured down 1200 feet without reaching bottom, at a site now known to be 12,000 feet deep. After Magellan was killed at Cebu in the Philippines, his ship, commanded by Juan del Cano, completed the first circumnavigation of the globe. This feat demonstrated to the world not only how vast the oceans were and how much was yet to be explored but also that the circumnavigation of the earth was possible.

What events in the late eighteenth and early nineteenth centuries influenced marine science and engineering?

The first organized attempts to study the world's oceans took place late in the eighteenth century. Perhaps not surprisingly—considering his many other accomplishments— Benjamin Franklin was the first person to plot the course of the Gulf Stream. This he did by systematically measuring the water temperature while crossing the Atlantic, and he found that the Gulf Stream was a strong east-flowing current. In 1770, Franklin published his findings and suggested that ship captains take advantage of this North Atlantic current (as he called the Gulf Stream) when sailing east and avoid it when sailing west.

Thomas Truxton, who was named by President George Washington as one of the first six U.S. Navy captains, was inspired by

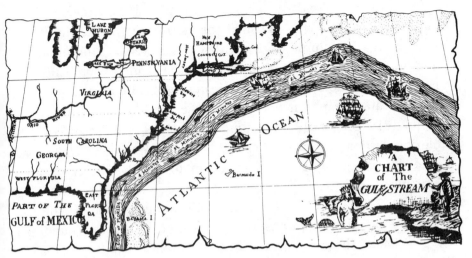

Benjamin Franklin's chart of the Gulf Stream.

Franklin's work and so decided to expand on it. Accordingly, in 1794, he published a manual of navigation that was based on his own, still-valid observations and principles.

In 1768, the English naval officer James Cook sailed around New Zealand, and between 1772 and 1775 he circumnavigated Antarctica and discovered the South Sandwich Islands (present-day Hawaii). Cook recorded subsurface temperatures and took soundings down to 4000 feet. He also brought ocean science into some prominence by taking along on these expeditions Sir Joseph Banks, an eminent natural historian, and William Wales and William Bayly, both astronomers. Their contributions were so impressive that subsequently many ships sent on extended voyages of exploration took scientists along. Charles Darwin was one such an (unpaid and usually seasick) individual who went with the survey ship *Beagle* in 1831. From the data he collected, he developed his revolutionary—and evolutionary—theory on the origin of species.

Alexander Von Humboldt (1769–1859), a German, was inspired by the Cook expeditions and so made a five-year (1799–

1804) voyage to Cuba, Mexico, and many places along the coast of Latin America. He published the results of this scientific journey in a 17-volume work entitled *The Travels of Humboldt and Bonpland in the Interior of America,* which established Humboldt as one of the period's greatest scientific contributors to physical geography, meteorology, and oceanography.

In 1818, Sir John Ross, commanding HMS *Isabella* and exploring Baffins Bay (an arm of the North Atlantic near Greenland) for the purpose of "inquiring in to the Possibility of a Northwest Passage," recovered bottom mud from depths of 1000 fathoms (73° 37' N, 77° 25' W) and 1050 fathoms. Although this was a remarkable accomplishment, it was not a deep-sea sounding, because the deep oceans have an average depth of 2555 fathoms, or more than 2.5 miles. Between 1819 and 1821, the Russian admiral Thaddeus Bellingshausen circumnavigated the southern polar ocean and made valuable observations of the region, as did George Powell, an English sea captain whose primary mission in 1821 was to hunt for seals. Powell observed, among other things, that in the Antarctic, just as in the Arctic, there is a layer of warm water below the cold-water surface. In 1823, another English sealer, James Weddell, sailed to the Antarctic and measured water temperatures in the region.

Sir James Clark Ross of Britain, the most accomplished polar explorer of the nineteenth century, led a national expedition in 1839–1843 to the Antarctic, with instructions to take deep-ocean temperatures, collect biological specimens, and conduct research in geology, tides, magnetism, and meteorology. Ross took depth measurements reportedly as deep as 16,062 feet some 450 miles west of the Cape of Good Hope. J. D. Hooker, who sailed with Ross, published his findings on marine biology, in which he described some 230 fishes, of which 145 were new to science.

Finally, Edward Forbes (1815–1845), an Englishman, professional scientist, and teacher, made many contributions to this period's knowledge of marine biology. He is remembered especially for his 1835–1841 investigations, including those while on the British survey ship HMS *Beacon*, relating the influence of the chemistry and physics of the ocean to marine life, and for improving on dredge designs used to collect deep ocean-bottom life samples. Ironically, despite his contributions, Forbes is also remembered for his erroneous theory that no life could exist in the ocean below about 1800 feet. The water pressures in the deep ocean made this theory plausible: The more water there is above something, the greater will be the weight pressing down on it. For example, one cubic foot of water weighs over 60 pounds, and for every 33 feet of depth the pressure increases by almost 15 pounds per square inch. Creatures living at 330 feet below sea level thus must be able to withstand 150 pounds of pressure per square inch of body surface, and at 3300 feet this increases to more than 1500 pounds. Anything living in the deepest parts of the ocean—33,000 to 36,000 feet below sea level—must survive 7.5 tons pushing down on every part of its body, and we know now that life exists at these depths.

Who was the first modern oceanographer?

For all intents and purposes, U.S. Navy lieutenant Matthew Fontaine Maury (1806–1873) is generally recognized by Americans as the father of modern-day physical oceanography. He was known to be a strong-willed, self-assured, controversial individual who placed the interests of the navy ahead of those for the advancement of science. This was the opinion of the scientists of the time such as Joseph Henry and Alexander Bache, who considered Maury to be an amateur and to lack the training and professionalism of a competent scientist. Even though they acknowledged Maury's work as inventive, they believed it to be seriously flawed in many aspects.

Maury entered the navy as a midshipman in 1825 and served at sea until 1834. In 1834 and 1836, he published two papers on navigation that won the approval of both sailors and scientists. However, differences of opinion and squabbles between U.S. Navy lieutenant Charles Wilkes and Maury on the types of research to be carried out by the United States Exploring Expedition of 1838–1842, which was authorized by Congress and commanded by Wilkes, prevented Maury from participating. This scientific expedition (perhaps the greatest, albeit the least known, ever launched by the United States) was charged with "exploring and surveying the Pacific Ocean and the South Seas in order to promote the interests of commerce and navigation and the extension of scientific knowledge." Although much of the marine biology and many of the oceanographic results of this expedition were never published, an atlas with maps of the Antarctic continent, the Fiji Islands, and Hawaii and information on celestial navigation rates as a classic of scientific exploration.

After being hurt in a stagecoach accident in 1839, Maury was appointed in 1842 as the officer in charge of the navy's Depot of Charts and Instruments. In his 19 years as head of this office, Maury systematically collected information from naval vessels and merchantmen on currents, weather, winds, and other useful data found in ships' logs. Charts and notices to mariners based on this information soon became popular with both naval and merchant marine personnel throughout the world. In 1855, Maury published what may be the first textbook on oceanography, *The Physical Geography of the Sea*, which won world acclaim. Although some of its information was erroneous and was challenged by scientists of the time and later, Maury's initiative and systematic methods of compiling and using data were generally well regarded. Such methods stimulated international cooperation in oceanography, a cooperation that Maury encouraged. He was concerned, as well, with the practical application of oceanography and should also be considered as a significant pioneer in ocean engineering and marine geology because of his

Lieutenant Matthew Fontaine Maury. *(Courtesy U.S. Navy)*

investigations of the ocean floor in support of Cyrus W. Field's North Atlantic cable project.

Field was a wealthy American industrialist who was interested in installing an Atlantic telegraph cable on the floor of the Atlantic Ocean, a region then almost entirely unknown. He asked Maury for advice on the proposed project. In response, Maury drew the first (bathymetric) map of the North Atlantic ocean floor, with the aid of a simple but revolutionary new apparatus called the Deep Sea Sounding Device, which had been invented in 1852 by a Maury protégé, navy midshipman John Mercer Brooke. The map showed a plateau, the telegraphic plateau, as Maury called it, between Ireland and New Foundland. Relying on this information and Maury's judgment that the project was feasible, Field began in mid-1857 to have the cable laid and it was put into service several years later in 1866.

When did scientific oceanography begin?

Oceanography received its greatest impetus from the British navy's 1872–1876 expedition by the three-masted, square-rigged wooden ship the HMS *Challenger*. Under the leadership of C. Wyville Thomson, it covered some 69,000 miles and investigated 362 ocean sites. It was the first deep-ocean global expedition ever attempted. Biological specimens, water, and bottom samples were collected, and ocean currents and temperatures were measured. Sir John Murray's report in 1895 described the main outlines of the ocean basins and provided a huge amount of new information about marine life and marine geology. For instance, the analysis of the samples of the ocean bottom laid the foundation of geological oceanography. In addition, the 77 ocean water samples proved for the first time that various constituents of the oceans water's salts maintain virtually the same proportions everywhere, although not at every depth.

Largely because of the *Challenger's* success, several more oceanic expeditions were made, and oceanic institutions were established. To name but a few: The Alexander Agassiz 1877–1905 voyages of the Caribbean, Gulf of Mexico, and Pacific were made on the *Albatross*, the first ship designed and built specifically for oceanographic research; the Marine Biological Laboratory in Bristol, England, was founded in 1879; the German expedition of 1889 in the North Atlantic, the voyage under the direction of Professor Victor Hensen in the SS *National*, was made to study the floating microscopic life on the ocean surface, which Hensen named *plankton*; the Oceanographic Museum

HMS *Challenger.*

and Laboratory was opened in Monaco in 1906, and the Scripps Institution of Oceanography was opened in San Diego in 1905; and the around-the-world cruise of the Russian ship *Vitiaz* was made during 1886–1889 to measure various ocean temperatures and densities particularly in the North Pacific. Between 1917 and 1941, the Woods Hole Oceanographic Institution (1930) and the Duke University Marine Laboratory and Narragansett Marine Laboratory (both 1937) were founded. Numerous ships of many nationalities also carried out ocean research investigations during this time. Among them were the Danish *Dana*, which during its voyages of 1920–1922 and 1928–1930 made important discoveries, including the breeding place of the European eels in the Sargasso Sea; the American *Carnegie's* expedition in 1927–1929; the German *Meteor's* chemical investigations of the Atlantic from 1928 to 1938; and the 1925 and 1930–1939 British *Discovery's* studies of Antarctic whales and their environment.

At the same time, research began on ocean currents, working out the details of the relationship of the ocean's chlorinity, salinity, and density, enabling the prevailing theories to be verified by field observations. The invention of the sonic depth finder in 1921 provided the means to determine more accurately the oceans' size and shape. And the founding in the same year of the International Hydrographic Bureau in Monaco formalized the free exchange of various kinds of oceanographic information, resulting in the coordination and standardization of hydrographic surveying and charting by maritime nations. (In 1985, the fifth edition of the *General Bathymetric Chart of the Oceans* was published under the auspices of the International Hydrographic Organization and the Intergovernmental Oceanographic Commission. The book divides the oceans and surrounding continents into 18 regional sections, giving detailed charts of the ocean floor for each. This fifth edition combines for the first time the results of traditional soundings with satellite data.)

How has the focus of ocean engineering activity and research changed during the twentieth century?

Before World War II, ocean engineering endeavors were mainly building ships, laying ocean cables, building piers and breakwaters, constructing bridges, dredging harbors, and building submersibles and ocean salvage equipment. All of these applications of engineering to the oceans, though significant, represent only the beginning of ocean engineering.

Moreover, this work was carried out by engineers who usually had little or no detailed knowledge of the ocean—its waves, storms, currents, geology, and chemical properties. And until the 1960s, there were no organized authentic data, either scientific or engineering, regarding actual and potential interactions of the ocean environment with the various kinds of hardware placed in the ocean.

During World War II, many nations were forced to design and build ocean structures and equipment and to devise techniques for waging war at sea. It was then that the knowledge gap between engineering and ocean science became most apparent. Although these were mainly military applications of ocean engineering, World War II left a legacy of scientific and technological capabilities as well as a recognition of the need for more ocean research and engineering. Until World War II, there was no significant national or public interest in this work; oceanography was regarded as a "poor relation" to the other sciences. Moreover, although a small number of U.S. industrial organizations had begun ocean engineering projects, they had difficulty justifying spending much money on them. But then, during the war, the importance of both oceanography and ocean engineering and their applications became apparent. The recognition of this need resulted in, among other things, the 1959 report of the National Academy of Sciences entitled "Oceanography—1960–1970."

In regard to this report, the President's Science Advisory Committee commented:

> It was apparent from the deliberations that the traditional concept of "oceanography" as a basic science had changed since the 1930s. While emphasizing oceanography as an interdisciplinary science, the report also covered such subjects as marine resource development, ocean engineering, and man's effect upon the ocean environment— all very "practical" concerns directly related to the National interest. Programs that had never been recognized as "oceanography" in its classical sense were considered: Marine biology; water pollution control; shellfish sanitation; recreation; and coastal and deep ocean engineering. "Oceanography" had been broadened to include many aspects of man's activities in or on the ocean.

This 1959 report was one of the studies responsible for bringing ocean work to the national forefront and also for launching work in both oceanography and ocean engineering. Also, the 1960s brought more sensitive radio and radar receivers, electronic computers, space satellites, and many other devices, several of which were used in oceanographic instrumentation, specially modified survey and research ships, ocean platforms, and other systems. But even though ocean engineering today has emerged from its infancy, it still has not reached maturity.

THE PHYSICAL OCEAN

There is a tide in the affairs of men, which taken at the flood, leads on to fortune; omitted, all the voyage of their life is bound in shallows and in miseries. On such a full sea are we now afloat, and we must take the current when it serves or lose our ventures.

Shakespeare

What is physical oceanography, and what do physical oceanographers do?

Physical oceanography is the study of the ocean's physics, with the goal of understanding its movement and structure; the interactions of the water with its two principal boundaries, air and sediment; and the relationship of the ocean to other branches of oceanography and to meteorology. On the "full sea" of instrumentation technology that oceanographers "are now afloat," we must gain a fuller understanding of the physical ocean or risk losing "our ventures."

Physical oceanographers study and describe the causes of the various motions of ocean waters: the currents, tides, winds, certain ocean events like upwellings (or the rising of water from a lower to a higher level), and the related distribution patterns of

17

water properties, such as temperature, salinity, and pressure. All of these plus the earth's rotation and the pull of the sun and the moon contribute to oceanic motions.

In studying these motions, physical oceanographers must deal with a viscous, inhomogeneous, highly stratified fluid, existing as a relatively thin film partially covering a rotating planet—the earth. The transport and energy processes that take place in this fluid vary in duration from microseconds to thousands of years. Many of these processes still are obscure and poorly understood.

What is the difference between an ocean and a sea?

The world ocean (singular) is an interconnecting body containing more than 326 million cubic miles of saltwater in the depressions of the earth's surface, which occupy some 142 million square miles.

This global ocean's component parts are five bodies of water, each large enough to warrant the name ocean. They are the (1) Pacific, (2) Atlantic, (3) Indian, (4) Antarctic or Southern, and (5) Arctic. The Pacific (with its components, the North and South Pacific) is the largest of these oceans, covering more than 63 million square miles. The Atlantic (and its components, the North and South Atlantic) occupies 32 million square miles. The Indian Ocean is 28 million square miles large. And the Antarctic and Arctic are almost equal in size (5 million square miles), with the seas making up the difference.

The term *sea* is frequently used interchangeably with *ocean*. For example, we hear of the global sea, the sea around us, and the high seas. But a sea is not strictly the same as an ocean: A sea can be a body of saltwater that lacks an outlet to the ocean. Examples of such inland seas are the Dead Sea (405 square miles), the

Earth's global ocean covers an area nine times that of the moon. *(Courtesy U.S. Navy)*

Caspian (163,000 square miles), the Salton Sea, (300 square miles), and the Sea of Azov (14,688 square miles). Seas are also classified as enclosed and partly enclosed. The enclosed connected with the ocean via a narrow channel. An example is the Mediterranean Sea, a near-landlocked sea bounded by the coasts of Europe, Africa, and Asia. Its only access to the Atlantic is through the narrow Strait of Gibraltar.

In contrast, partly enclosed seas have a much wider channel to the ocean. Both the North Sea and the Weddell Sea qualify as partly enclosed types. At last count, oceanographers recognized some 54 seas, both enclosed and partly enclosed.

The smallest partly enclosed coastal body of water is an *estuary* and cannot really qualify as a sea. It is the area in which a river meets the ocean, and therefore its water is brackish, or saltwater diluted with freshwater.

The ancient Greeks thought of their global ocean as an endless stream surrounding the border of the earth. Inside this ocean was the sea, namely, the Mediterranean, which was familiar to them as well as to the Romans, who called it *mare nostrum*, or "our sea."

What are the Seven Seas?

To the ancients, "seven" often meant "many," and before the fifteenth century the many seas of the world were seven: the Red Sea, the Mediterranean Sea, the Persian Gulf, the Black Sea, the Adriatic Sea, the Caspian Sea, and the Indian Ocean. Today, when the term *seven seas*, popularized by Rudyard Kipling, is used at all, the usual designations are the Arctic Ocean, Antarctic Ocean, Indian Ocean, North Atlantic Ocean, North Pacific Ocean, South Atlantic Ocean, and South Pacific Ocean. Thus, the old seven seas are really seven oceans.

What kinds of ocean currents are there, and what causes them?

There are two kinds of ocean currents, surface and subsurface. Not surprisingly, surface currents do not extend more than a few feet below the surface. Subsurface currents are those running below them. The Gulf Stream, however, may be said to be both surface and subsurface.

Ocean currents are produced and maintained by the rotation of the earth, the winds, and differences in water density. In addition, the depth of the water, the underwater topography, the location of the land, and the shape of the basin in which the current is flowing all affect the ocean's circulation.

The stress of wind blowing across the ocean causes the surface layer of water to move. This motion is then transmitted to each succeeding layer below the surface, but because of internal friction with the water, the rate of motion decreases with the depth. The current thus produced is called a *wind current*. Although there are many variables, a steady wind lasting for about 12 hours is generally needed to establish such a current.

A wind current does not flow in the direction of the wind, however, as it is deflected by the rotation of the earth. This deflection is toward the right in the Northern Hemisphere, and toward the left in the Southern Hemisphere. The (Coriolis) force is greater in higher latitudes, and the difference between wind direction and surface wind—current direction usually varies from about 15 degrees along shallow coastal areas to a maximum of 45 degrees in the deep oceans. The angle increases with depth, and so at various depths the current may flow in the direction opposite to that of the surface current.

Many ocean currents help determine the climate of the coastal regions along which they flow. For example, warm water from the Gulf Stream—which later becomes the North Atlantic, the northeast drift, and the Irminger currents—travels all the

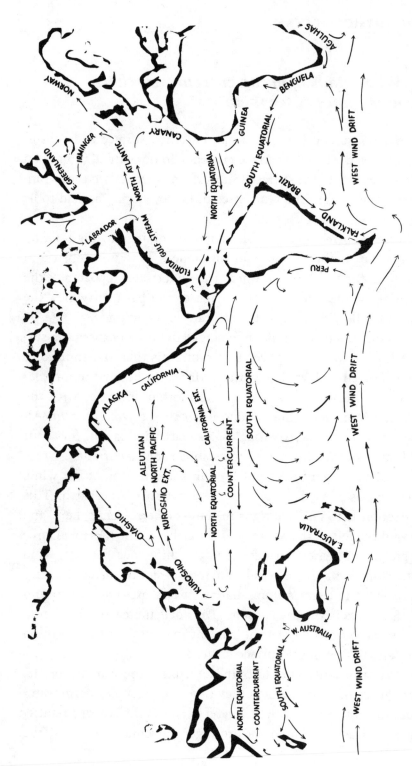

The world's major ocean currents. (*Courtesy Bureau of Commercial Fisheries*)

way to the southwest coast of Iceland, warming it to the extent that Reykjavik has a higher average winter temperature than does New York City, far to the south. Likewise, both Great Britain and Labrador are at about the same latitude, but Great Britain's climate is much milder than Labrador's because of the difference in temperature of their offshore currents. The West Coast of the United States is cooled in the summer by the California current and warmed in the winter by the Davidson current. Partly as a result of this condition, the range of monthly average temperatures on the West Coast is comparatively small.

Currents also affect the earth's pressure pattern, as the air over a cold current contracts as it is cooled, and that over a warm current expands as it is warmed. And as air cools above a cold ocean current, fog is likely to form. Frost smoke is most commonly found over a warm current that flows into a colder region, because evaporation is greater from warm water than from cold water.

Cooling air over the California current forms the fog in San Francisco's bay.
(Courtesy NOAA)

What is the Gulf Stream?

The Gulf Stream has often been referred to as a "river in the ocean." This "river" of ocean water generally follows the east coast of North America, flowing around Florida northeastward toward Cape Hatteras and then curving toward the east and becoming slower and broader. After passing the Grand Banks area, it turns slightly northward toward the North Atlantic and flows across it. The friction from permanent wind systems appears to be the most important factor in determining the Gulf Stream's motion in the North Atlantic Ocean, with northeast trade winds blowing across the southern part and prevailing westerlies across the northern part.

A tremendous volume of water flows northward in the Gulf Stream. It can be distinguished by its deep indigo-blue color, which contrasts sharply with the dull green of the surrounding water, and it is frequently accompanied by squalls. When the Gulf Stream encounters the cold water of the Labrador current, principally in the vicinity of the Grand Banks, there is little mixing of the waters; instead, the junction is marked by a sharp change in temperature.

Investigations have shown that the Gulf Stream itself is much narrower and faster than previously supposed and is considerably more variable in its position and speed. The maximum current off Florida ranges from about two to four knots. (A knot is one nautical mile—6112 feet—an hour.) Northward, the speed is generally less, and after the current passes Cape Hatteras, it decreases even further. As the stream meanders and shifts position, parts of it sometimes break off and continue as separate, circular flows until they dissipate.

Tidal forces apparently influence the Gulf Stream, which reaches its daily maximum speed about three hours after the transit of the moon. That is, when the moon is over the equator, the stream is narrower and faster than it is at its maximum

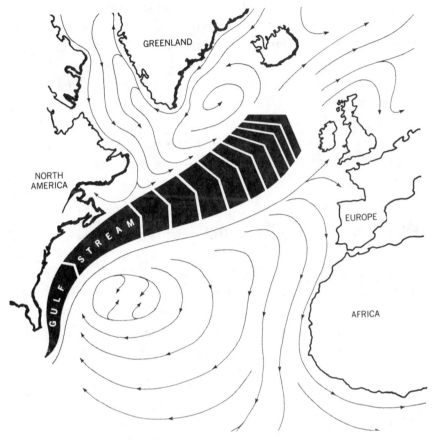

The Gulf Stream. *(Courtesy U.S. Navy)*

northerly or southerly declination. Variations in the trade winds also affect the current.

In past centuries, ocean sailors often discovered that they had been pushed off course or delayed by the Gulf Stream and so sought another, albeit longer, route. Recognizing the problem, Benjamin Franklin—who had studied the Gulf Stream—suggested to the British (before the Revolution, of course) that their ships travel through the Gulf Stream only from the American colonies back to England. In this way they could take advantage of the current and favorable winds to shorten their voyages. Previously, British ships had always used the northern route in both directions, losing a great deal of time from east to west, especially in unfavorable weather. Nonetheless, they ignored Franklin's advice—to their own detriment. Undeterred, Franklin drew a chart of the Gulf Stream's surface currents.

Franklin's chart, however, makes the pattern of currents look much simpler than it actually is; we know now that the Gulf Stream is highly complex and variable. It is not fixed in time and space, as is a river with which it has been compared, but changes, with the amount of change varying from time to time.

What is the Cromwell current?

The Cromwell current, named after Townsend Cromwell who discovered it in 1952, is a subsurface current that flows eastward beneath the equator in the Pacific Ocean. It is about 200 miles wide and about 700 feet deep, flowing west to east along the equator at 3.5 knots (or 3.5 nautical miles) per hour.

What is a thermocline?

Below the ocean's top sun-warmed layer is a much denser and colder (50° F) layer. The two do not mix easily, and where they meet is called the *thermocline,* or layer of discontinuity. Thermoclines can be either permanent or temporary. Permanent thermoclines normally occur at around 500 feet, except at around the equator where they are closer to the surface. Temporary thermoclines also are usually near the surface, although they may vary in depth or disappear depending on atmospheric conditions above the water. Below the thermoclines, water temperatures decrease slowly to about 35 to 37° F in most deep-ocean bottoms. Thermoclines, incidentally, distort the sound waves transmitted by echo sounders, a valuable tool used in oceanographic research.

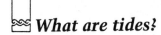 What are tides?

Tides are the periodic rising and falling of the oceans. The tides are typically 2 to 10 feet high but can also reach 50 or more feet in extreme cases, such as in the Bay of Fundy, in Canada.

How many kinds of tides are there?

There are three types of tides:

1. The twice-daily, or *semidiurnal*, tide has two high waters and two low waters each day, with little or no difference between consecutive high or low-water heights. Tides along the east coast of the United States, for example, are of the semidiurnal type.

2. The daily, or *diurnal*, tide has only one high water and one low water each day. The tides along the Vietnam-China coast are diurnal.

3. The *mixed* tide has both diurnal and semidiurnal characteristics. That is, there are two high waters and two low waters each day, but with a considerable difference between the heights of successive high waters or successive low waters; these differences are called *diurnal* (or daily) inequalities. The tides along the Pacific coast of the United States are of the mixed type.

What causes tides?

Tides are caused principally by the differences in the gravitational pull of the moon and sun on different parts of the rotating earth. The tide-producing force on the earth's hemisphere nearer the moon is in the direction toward the moon and its attraction.

The direction of tide-producing forces in relation to the moon's position around the equatorial plane.

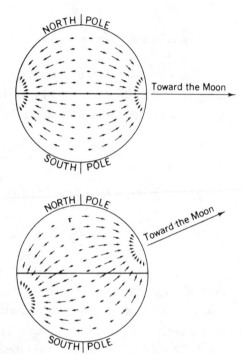

On the hemisphere opposite the moon the tide-producing force is in the direction of the centrifugal force or away from the moon.

In effect, the tide-producing forces tend to create high tides on the sides of the earth both nearest to and farthest from the moon, with a low tide belt between them. At those times of new moon and full moon, the sun's attraction adds to that of the moon, producing higher (spring) tides. These so-called spring tides are said to occur when the water springs up (the term *spring* has nothing to do with the season of the year). Halfway between a new and full moon, the sun's attraction does not coincide with that of the moon, and therefore the difference between the high and low tides is smaller. Such tides are called *neap* tides.

As the earth rotates, if the moon is over the equator, a point on earth will pass through two high and two low areas each day. When the moon is north or south of the equator, the two highs will be unequal in height, or there may be only one high tide.

Thus, changes in the moon's declination will cause a diurnal inequality in the pattern of the tidal forces at a particular place. Similar forces are exerted by the sun, and the total tide-producing force is the result of the two. Other celestial bodies have very small tidal effects.

Although the tide-producing forces are distributed over the earth fairly evenly, the sizes and shapes of the ocean basins and the interference of the landmasses prevent the oceans' tides from assuming a simple, regular pattern. The way in which the waters in different parts of the oceans, as well as in the smaller waterways, respond to these known, regular forces depends in large part on the size, depth, and configuration of the basin or waterway. For example, in some restricted water areas, such as bays and channels, the tide's height may rise to 50 feet or more. Tides moving upstream in an estuary are slowed down by bottom friction, and the flowing water builds up more rapidly than it falls. Areas of great tidal ranges are the Sea of Okhotsk and the Bay of Fundy. Conversely, areas such as the Gulf of Mexico and the Baltic, Mediterranean, and Adriatic seas have almost no tide.

In the United States, the National Ocean Survey, a component of the National Oceanic and Atmospheric Administration of the U.S. Department of Commerce, publishes each year the times and heights of high and low water.

What causes waves?

Waves on the surface of the ocean differ fundamentally from waves within the ocean. Surface waves are generated by the wind, and surface currents are influenced by the augmenting and opposing effects of the wind. Waves within the ocean, or *internal* waves, have various causes, such as tides, interactions among waves, and atmospheric disturbances. They are characterized by their slow progressive oscillations, which range up to hundreds

Ocean surface waves. *(Courtesy U.S. Coast Guard)*

of miles. The internal waves in the Sulu Sea, southwest of the Philippine Islands, appear to be the longest anywhere in the world. They have been investigated by oceanographers using subsurface current-measuring devices, acoustic echo sounders, and towed thermistor chains.

What was the highest open-ocean wave ever recorded?

There may have been ocean waves higher than the one some 112 feet high that was measured in 1933 by the American tanker USS *Ramapo* during a 68-knot windstorm en route from Manila to San Diego, but they were not officially recorded. Most of the familiar ocean waves generated by the force of the wind—such as ripples, swell, chop, and surf—are generally less than 12 feet high. Waves over 50 feet high occur only during very severe storms.

What causes tidal waves?

The so-called tidal waves are not caused by tides but, rather, by disturbances associated with earthquakes occurring below or near the ocean floor. They are more correctly termed *tsunami* (Japanese for "harbor wave"). A tsunami is a series of traveling ocean waves of extremely long length and duration. As the tsunami crosses the deep ocean, its length from crest to crest may be a hundred miles or more, with a height from trough to crest of only a few feet. It cannot be felt aboard ships in deep water and cannot be seen from the air. But in deep water, a tsunami may reach a forward speed of more than 600 miles per hour.

As the tsunami enters the shoaling water of the coastlines in its path, the velocity of its waves diminishes, and its wave height increases. It is in these shallow waters that the tsunami can become a threat to life and property, for it can crest to heights of more than 100 feet and strike with devastating force.

◳ *What is a rip current?*

When tides, wind-generated waves, and waves caused by the bow of a ship moving through the water break at an angle to the coast, some of the energy goes into a long-shore current that flows along the beach in the surf zone. The waves that continually add water to this current increase its transport until it overflows and returns seaward through the breakers in a strong flow called a *rip current*. The long-shore and rip currents together constitute a near-shore circulation system. The dissipation of wave energy on the sandy bottom supplies the power for setting sediments in motion, whereas the long-shore and rip currents produce a net transport of sediment.

◳ *What are the deepest parts of the ocean?*

The average depth of the oceans is about five times the average elevation of the land, and in general, the continents stand about three miles above the ocean floor. In 1962, a depth of 35,800 feet was recorded in the deepest-known part of the ocean, the Mindanao Trench east of the Philippine Islands. If the world's highest mountain, Mount Everest (29,141 feet) were to be placed into this trench, it would be covered by over a mile and a quarter of water.

◳ *Where did the water in the ocean come from?*

Some scientists believe that the oceans originally contained only about 16 percent of their current volume (326 million cubic miles). This probably came from water vapor in the atmosphere and later from water in rocks that was released during the earth's formation. Rainwater was released from clouds in the atmosphere, and as the earth cooled, more water came up from volcanoes, hot springs, and other sources and gradually filled the oceans.

Why is the ocean blue?

The ocean often looks blue because of sun's shining on tiny particles suspended in the water. But along the shores of some areas, the water looks green, because of the blue water's being mixed with the yellow pigments present in floating plants. Although the water in the open ocean and in the Gulf Stream off the east coast of Florida is blue, a current off Japan is called the Kuroshio, or the "black stream," because it is so dark. The Black Sea looks black because it has little oxygen and a high concentration of hydrogen sulphide. The Red Sea is red because it contains seasonal blooms of algae that color the surface water red. And the Yellow Sea is yellow because it contains a yellow mud carried into it by adjoining rivers.

What does the term "horse latitudes" mean?

In the horse latitudes, whose latitude is 30° N and 30° S, the ocean is often calm because of the absence of winds. Apparently, the area received its name because sailing ships carrying horses across the Atlantic were often becalmed or unable to move. After running out of sufficient fodder for the horses, they were forced to throw them overboard.

How do oceanographers study the ocean's structure and movement?

Oceanographers first measure various aspects of the ocean, such as its salinity, density, depth, and temperatures; dynamic properties caused by waves, currents, and tides; winds and humidity; chemical properties; and bottom and subbottom geology. Most of the instruments to make such measurements require the extensive use of sensors—by aircraft, helicopters, satellites, buoys, and ships—to collect physical chemical, biological, and other information simultaneously and over large areas.

There are now about 21,000 instruments of 34 generic types used for sensing and sampling the ocean. Many of these are

A Nansen bottle.

multipurpose devices that can be used for physical, biological, geological, chemical, and meteorological ocean research measurements. Such instrument systems usually contain (1) related equipment to support the instrument, (2) sensors, (3) a power supply, and (4) a subsystem to record, store, and transmit data. The following four instruments are typical of those now being used by physical oceanographers:

Nansen or Nisken bottles. A traditional method of taking ocean water samples at various depths and locations is by means of Nansen or Nisken bottles. They are lowered into the ocean on a cable and are opened, either electronically or mechanically, at a certain depth. The bottles (Nisken types are more often used) are then brought aboard, and the water samples are analyzed in the shipboard laboratory.

Current meters. Instruments to measure the velocity and direction of ocean currents are usually attached to buoys or moorings. The instrument's basic components are a rotor to sense the water's speed, and a vane to sense its direction. Recorders average the frequent direction changes, and sensors using acoustics and magnetic techniques measure the current's flow and direction.

Satellites now can obtain much vital oceanographic information. When they contain the proper mix of sensors—infrared, microwave imaging, microwave radiometers, altimeters, and scatterometers (for global surface wind data)—satellites can accurately analyze ocean surface environments, showing the position of ocean fronts under all weather conditions, around the world, and during both night and day.

Another measuring technique, developed by Dr. Walter Munk of the Scripps Institution of Oceanography and Dr. Carl Wunsch of the Massachusetts Institute of Technology, is called *ocean acoustic tomography.* In this experimental technique, an acoustic pulse or "ping" is sent out from one of three ocean buoys located in a triangular pattern some 600 miles on each side. The signal travels through the water to the receiving buoy, and from

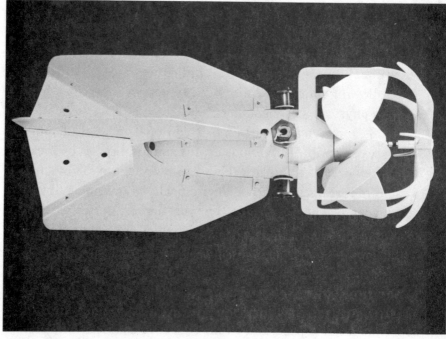

A radio current meter. *(Courtesy NOAA)*

an analysis of the arrival of the pulses, it is possible to determine the water conditions at various depths and to map the ocean in three dimensions. That is, the signal's velocity depends on the surrounding water's temperature, salinity, and pressure. With additional technology and more buoys, it would theoretically be possible, with the aid of computers, to map ocean motions and temperatures throughout the huge world ocean.

Temperature profilers. Electronic temperature depth recorders monitor the ocean's upper-layer thermal structure. They have a radio link so that the temperature—depth unit (AXBT) can be dropped from an aircraft recording the data. The recorder with a wire link (XBT) dropped from a surface ship has a thermistor to sense the temperature and to calculate the depth by the fall rate of the unit into the water.

Velocity profiles. To measure a current's depth—in order to understand better the ocean's circulation—a sinking float, a free-fall device, or a attached profiler may be used. The sinking float is tracked acoustically as it sinks, and its path is mapped so as to show velocity and thereby depth. The free-fall device contains a current sensor, and the attached profiler has a current meter on a line attached to a buoy or a ship. New techniques such as the acoustic doppler profiler (ADP) can overcome some of the shortcomings of the velocity profilers in large-scale experiments and survey programs.

The experiments with ocean acoustic tomography are in preparation for the World Ocean Circulation Experiment scheduled for 1990 to 1995. This project, in which virtually all of the

A temperature sensor.

world's maritime nations will participate, will use ships, satellites, and buoys equipped with a wide range of instrumentation. The project's specific aim, which will be carried out with other programs such as the Global Ocean Flux Study and the Tropical Ocean Global Atmosphere Programs, is to chart the world ocean's general circulation so that changes in the circulation that accompany changes in the climate can be recognized, monitored, and modeled.

THE CHEMICAL OCEAN

The planet earth is misnamed, if you consider it from the proportion of land to water. By a fair naming process it would be called planet water.

John and Mildred Teal,
The Sargasso Sea

 What is chemical oceanography?

Chemical oceanography is the chemical mapping of the ocean. For a more specific answer, the broad field of chemistry can be divided into organic chemistry, or the chemistry of carbon compounds (especially those occurring in plants and animals), and inorganic chemistry, the chemistry of the compounds of elements other than carbon. Each of these branches deals, in part, with the discovery and tabulation of chemical facts (descriptive chemistry) and, in part, with the formulation of theories that, when proven, link these facts together into a plan or system (theoretical chemistry). Organic chemistry and inorganic chemistry can be further divided into, for example, analytical chemistry, physical chemistry, biochemistry, nuclear chemistry, and industrial chemistry. All these chemical specialities are used

39

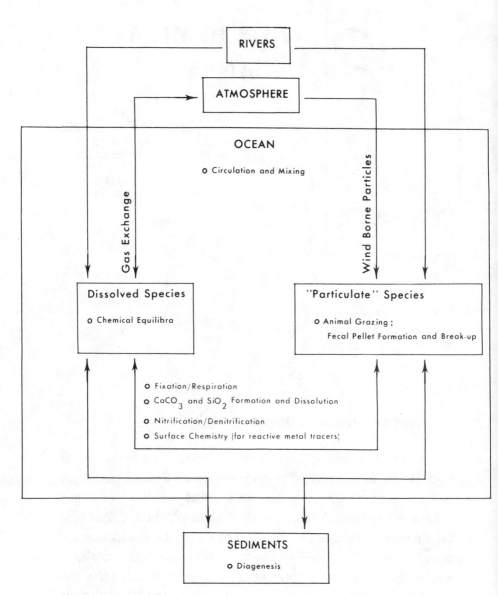

The ocean's carbon cycle.

in ocean-mapping studies, with analytical chemistry being the most often used.

Why is an understanding of the ocean's chemistry valuable?

We can apply our understanding of the ocean's chemistry to many global needs: providing food for the earth's expanding population, finding new sources of energy, improving health and conquering disease, discovering substitutes for scarce and dwindling resources, strengthening national security, and monitoring and protecting our environment.

For example, first, mining of the ocean may one day become an economic reality. Seawater itself is an ore of many materials, such as magnesium, bromine, and uranium, and mining such deposits in solution will rely heavily on chemists and chemical engineers. Second, marine chemistry studies may contribute to the ocean's productive potential. All living things in the ocean depend for their existence on the presence of sufficient quantities of chemical nutrients in the sunlit surface waters to permit the growth and productivity of marine phytoplankton. These single-cell algae are by far the most abundant type of ocean plant, and they are the most important link in the food web supporting marine animal life. The rate of supply and replenishment of nutrients through physical, chemical, biological processes thus directly affects the productivity of an ocean region.

Chemical oceanographers evaluate the damaging effects of harmful or toxic substances released as a result of industrial waste disposal, agricultural chemical runoff, and ocean dumping. Toxins contained in the various industrial wastes dumped into the oceans appear to have been responsible for the death of many whales, porpoises, seals, and fish during 1988 in the Baltic and North seas and off Cape Cod, Massachusetts. Some toxins that are dangerous to human health or marine organisms may now exist in concentrations that still cannot be detected by even the more sensitive techniques of chemical analysis currently available.

Chemical oceanographers also evaluate areas known to be affected by pollution from nontoxic, organic industrial and agricultural waste and sewage. One such condition is known as *eutrophication.* This results in the overstimulation of phytoplankton blooms, which in turn results in an accumulation of decaying plant matter and the depletion of the water's oxygen. Without sufficient oxygen, the ocean cannot support most animal life, including pelagic (free-swimming) and bottom-feeding fishes, and many kinds of shellfish.

What do chemical oceanographers use to study the ocean?

The tools of marine chemists are similar to those of chemists working in any other environment, with the addition of certain specialized techniques designed to identify and evaluate particular reactions and processes as they occur in the ocean. The sampling methods are often the same as those that physical oceanographers use. For example, the collection of water from various depths such sampling devices as (Nisken) bottles are used. In fact, some chemical, physical, and biological analyses use the same set of samples. However, the types of analyses used to answer questions about chemical oceanographic processes are different from those required for physical oceanographic studies. They range from relatively simple measurements such as an evaluation of the water's oxygen content, to extremely sensitive and complex measurements of substances that occur in very low concentrations, quickly degrade, and combine with other natural substances or change when in contact with certain types of sampling equipment. Although new instruments have been developed to perform chemical analyses at sea, some of the more sensitive measurements require both temperature-controlled transport of samples to land-based laboratory facilities and the availability of very sensitive analytical equipment.

Since the 1970s, there have been important developments in marine chemistry instrumentation, especially the addition of minicomputers and microprocessors to chemical sensors to form "intelligent" chemical instruments.

How old is the study of chemical oceanography?

Marine chemistry or chemical oceanography became a recognized division of chemistry only recently. In the past, scientists from several disciplines used the techniques and principles of chemistry to study the ocean's properties, but much of the information they obtained was of greater interest to biological and physical oceanographers than to chemists. Even now, there is no branch of oceanography that is not in some way dependent on chemical information and techniques. Marine chemists in the future will have better instruments to study the ocean, in collaboration with scientists of many disciplines.

How is chemical oceanography used?

Ocean water is a solution of strong electrolytes (dissolved compounds that conduct an electric current), gases, and organic compounds, and chemical oceanography is basically the study of the chemical properties of this solution, the cause and effect of variations of these properties with time and from place to place, and their measurements. Accordingly, chemical engineers are seeking ways to obtain, economically, fresh drinking water from the ocean, by distilling the seawater, perhaps, or in some other way removing the salt. Other engineers are trying to control seawater's costly corrosion. Another promising area for chemical oceanography is protecting the ocean's food supply.

Both engineers and environmentalists are working to increase the world's food supply: The ocean waters absorb more than two-thirds of the solar energy available for photosynthesis. (Photosynthesis is the process in nature by which green plants, algae, and photosynthetic bacteria use sunlight to change carbon dioxide and water into organic compounds, some of which are stored in the plants to provide energy for other forms of life.) Even though photosynthesis converts each year about a trillion tons of carbon into organic compounds, the total amount of the earth's stored energy in the form of hydrocarbons is decreasing while the carbon dioxide in the atmosphere is increasing. Such changes are due to the huge amounts of energy that people consume—yet another need for better understanding the chemistry underlying photosynthesis.

Chemists can also contribute their expertise to solve another problem; stopping the destruction of potential food from the ocean. Currently, the harvest of fish, mollusks (clams, oysters, mussels), and crustaceans (crabs, lobsters, shrimp) has decreased because of the dumping of harmful wastes into various parts of the oceans. Chemical oceanographic research can be helpful to mariculture (fish farming) and the protection of these food resources, by identifying effects of various wastes on the marine environment or the marine resources.

What is the composition, or "chemistry", of the ocean?

The ocean contains every known naturally occurring element plus various gases, chemical compounds, and minerals. The ocean's principal dissolved solids are the sodium salts (sodium chloride, or common salt), calcium (calcium carbonate, or

A Bodman water sampler.

lime, and calcium sulphate), potassium (potassium sulphate), and magnesium (magnesium chloride, magnesium sulphate, and magnesium bromide). There are varying, lesser amounts of bromine, strontium, boron, fluorine, barium, iodine, arsenic, silver, gold, rubidium, manganese, copper, lead, zinc, and uranium. It has been estimated that if the ocean's total salt content were dried, it would form another continent of solid salt the size of Africa. Furthermore, if mined, the gold suspended in seawater would give every person on earth nine pounds. And, in each cubic yard of seawater there is at least 32 ounces of magnesium, 2 ounces of bromine, 10 ounces of calcium, 22 ounces of sulpher, 10 ounces of potassium, 730 ounces of calcium chloride, and several others.

The ocean also contains organic substances and particulate matter (both sediment particles and the remains of decaying plants and animals). In addition, the ocean is, unfortunately, the final resting place of various substances such as sewage, oil, and pesticides. We do not yet know their full effects.

What gases does the ocean contain?

Ocean water contains all the gases found in the atmosphere, but not in the same proportion. Oxygen, nitrogen, and carbon dioxide are relatively abundant, with the other gases accounting for only about 0.25 percent, by weight.

Nitrogen is the most abundant gas in the ocean, and it is present as both a free dissolved gas and in various compounds (nitrate, nitrite, and ammonia). The bottom sediments contain small amounts of organic nitrogen.

Oxygen is produced in the ocean's surface layers by means of plant photosynthesis or is dissolved directly from the atmosphere. Its concentration varies from place to place, although the entire ocean is aerobic (contains oxygen). The concentration

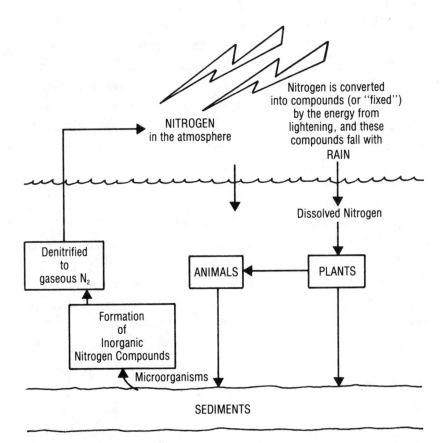

The ocean's nitrogen cycle.

of oxygen below the surface is usually only a fraction of the surface amounts, and under certain conditions—owing to the presence of abundant oxidizable materials, a stagnant condition, or both—it may be absent altogether.

Under such conditions, sulfate-reducing bacteria produce hydrogen sulfide gas from the abundant sulfate in the water. This hydrogen sulfide may also be present in deep ocean waters. In the Black Sea, the Bosporus and Dardanelles act as barriers, or sills, cutting off the deeper water from contact with the surface waters, which, diluted by the runoff from the Danube and Don rivers have a salinity of about 17.5 parts per thousand. The deeper water, renewed only by the bottom current through the Bosporus, has a salinity of 22 parts per thousand. The great difference in density between the surface layers and the deeper water effectively prevents the mixing and transfer of dissolved oxygen from the surface layers to the lower depths. Below about 100 fathoms, therefore, the waters of the Black Sea contain no dissolved oxygen, substituting instead large concentrations of hydrogen sulfide.

Carbon dioxide is formed in the ocean from the transfer of gases at the surface and from metabolic activities. To summarize the ocean's carbon cycle, the algae or small marine plants (phytoplankton) take up the dissolved carbon dioxide in the process of photosynthesis and then give off oxygen. The fish consume the carbon fixed by the plants, use the dissolved oxygen for respiration, and release carbon dioxide. When the ocean animals and plants decay and die, they give off carbon dioxide—a product of decay—which then returns to the atmosphere.

 How salty is seawater?

The amount of salt in more than 95 percent of the world's open ocean normally varies from 33 to 37 parts per thousand (or partial salinity units), with an average of about 35 (ppt). The northern subtropical portions of the Atlantic Ocean are very salty, 37.5 ppt. The Pacific Ocean is less salty (about 34 ppt. in its deeper areas), and the Arctic and Antarctic oceans are the least salty. Not surprisingly, the water is least salty where large quantities of freshwater are supplied by melting ice, rivers, or excessive rainfall. The most salty water is found in waters where there is a minimum of rainfall or river runoff, and high evaporation. For example, the Persian Gulf and the Red Sea have salinities of over 42 ppt.

A salinometer. *(Courtesy Woods Hole Oceanographic Institute [WHOI])*

How serious is the problem of ocean pollution today?

For the past 100 years, the ocean has been the largest dumping ground for wastes from ships, cities, and industries. But since 1972, the United States has prohibited industrial waste dumping in the open ocean (that part of the ocean outside the territorial jurisdiction of any country), and so the dumping of sewage sludge and dredged material is now relatively controlled. As a consequence, comparatively few problems caused by waste disposal in the open ocean have been documented. One reason for this is that whatever wastes are disposed of are usually dispersed and diluted, although we still are unable to determine exactly their impact on the open ocean.

In contrast, coastal waters and estuaries (semienclosed regions in which freshwater mixes with saltwater) have been hard hit by waste disposal practices. These areas receive most of the pollutants introduced into the marine environment, and yet there are no state and federal protection programs for most estuaries and coastal waters. As a result of this and the growing population in coastal areas, about 9 million tons of sewage sludge, 180 million metric tons of dredged material, and various wastes from some 1300 major industrial facilities and 600 municipal activities now are dumped annually in the fragile coastal waters and estuaries. The health of these waters, which are heavily used as a source of food and recreation, is now being seriously threatened. Commercial harvesting has been prohibited or restricted for about one-third of the productive shellfishing areas of the United States, and several beaches have been closed because of contamination.

As previously noted increasing concern over the adverse impact of ocean dumping led to passage of the Marine Protection, Research, and Sanctuaries Act of 1972 (PL 92-532); which states:

The dark shape off New York City is probably caused by chemical waste.
(Courtesy NOAA)

No person shall transport from the United States any radiological, chemical, or biological warfare agents . . . for the purpose of dumping into ocean waters. . . . No officer, employee, agent, department, agency, or instrumentality of the United States shall transport from any location outside the United States any radiological, chemical, or biological warfare agent . . . for the purpose of dumping it into ocean waters.

This act represented at least one forward step. But the world's ocean must be treated as an entity—inclusive of coastal zones and estuaries. Accordingly, the long-term protection of the world's ocean will be a greater focus of oceanographic research.

What is a red tide?

A red tide, with its mass fish kill, occurs when either natural or human factors cause a rapid increase in the production of one-celled organisms (dinoflagellates), which ordinarily grow in waters rich in nitrogen and phosphorus. These destructive red tides, also known as paralytic shellfish poisoning, have occurred since biblical times but are becoming much more prevalent today. Sewage effluent and runoff from farms and lawns contain nitrogen and phosphorus, and when added to the ocean, the dinoflagellates gobble them up and reproduce or "bloom" profusely and spread across the water like a carpet, absorbing oxygen and shutting off sunlight from plants. Then, when these organisms die and decay, they absorb more oxygen, literally suffocating marine life.

3 THE BIOLOGICAL OCEAN

Nature has no designs or intentions. All that live exist only because they have adapted themselves to the hard lines that nature has laid down.

Thomas H. Huxley

 What is biological oceanography?

Biological oceanography is the study of ocean organisms and how these forms of life, as a part of the total ocean system, interact with this environment and one another. Biological oceanographers study how oceanic environments affect the organisms' distribution, behavior, evolution, and life processes. Biological oceanography as a separate discipline is less than 200 years old. It is a branch of biology, which has two main divisions: botany, the study of plants, and zoology, the study of animals.

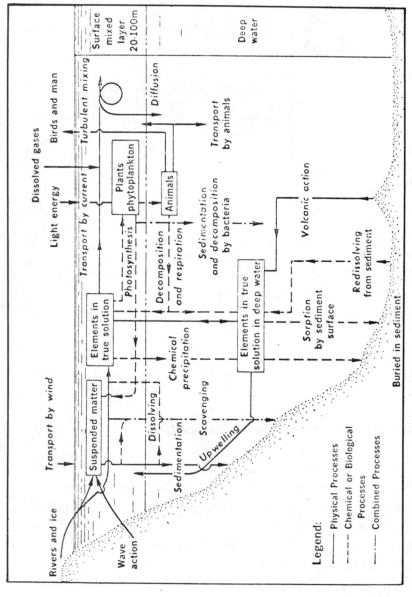

Life processes in the ocean. (*Courtesy U.S. Navy*)

What kinds of plants live in the ocean?

The smallest plants living in the ocean are *plankton*, which are all the tiny (varying in size from about 5 microns to 50 millimeters), floating marine plants and animals too weak to do anything but drift with the currents. They are the predominant form of life in the ocean. The plants are known as *phytoplankton*, and the animals are known as *zooplankton*. Both are important food sources for fish and other animals.

Single-celled plants, or *diatoms*, constitute more than half of the plankton in the ocean. These plants, together with the rest of the phytoplankton, are often referred to as "the grass of the

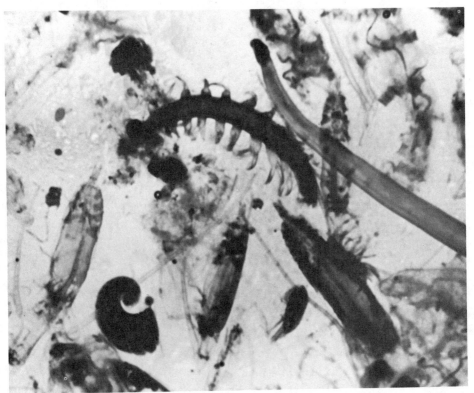

A photomicrographic view of plankton. *(Courtesy NOAA)*

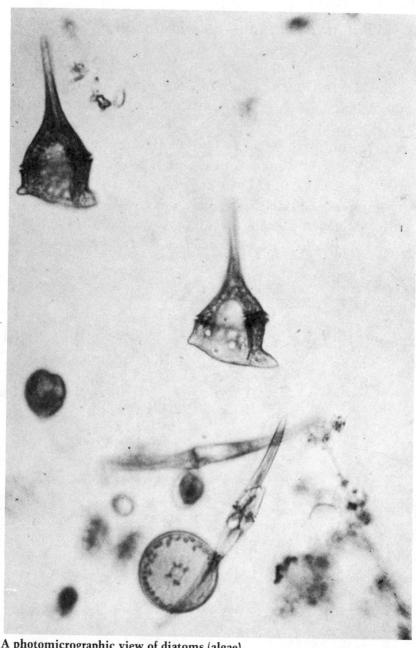

A photomicrographic view of diatoms (algae).

ocean." By means of photosynthesis they convert chemical nutrients such as the salts and minerals in the ocean water into their food. The phytoplankton, in turn, are consumed by the zooplankton and by some of the larger animals. Then the larger animals, such as fish, lobsters and crabs, feed on the zooplankton. The chemical nutrients are replaced in the ocean by the excretion of animals and bacterial action in the decomposition of dead plants and animals. Thus, the ocean's food cycle is continuous, from chemical nutrient to phytoplankton to zooplankton to strong swimming animals to chemical nutrient.

Phytoplankton need both sunlight and chemical nutrients to grow, but sunlight in sufficient strength to permit photosynthesis penetrates only to a maximum depth of about 500 to 600 feet. This upper layer of the ocean's water is called the *euphotic zone*. Within this zone, photosynthesis is limited by the supply of chemical nutrients. Under favorable conditions, phytoplankton may increase by as much as 300 percent in a single day, and a cubic foot of ocean water may contain 20,000 plants.

The abundance of marine life is directly related to the supply of phytoplankton. In shallow water, the chemical nutrients on the bottom are stirred up by motion of the water and carried into the euphotic zone, which is why an area such as the Grand Banks is a good fishing ground. In polar regions the chemical nutrients are relatively abundant, being brought to the surface by convective currents as the cold surface water sinks and is replaced by the warmer water from the bottom. In the tropics, on the other hand, the water is relatively stable, and so the chemical nutrients have a tendency to sink below the euphotic zone. Even though the clear, blue water has the deepest euphotic zone, photosynthesis proceeds at a slower rate there. For this reason, blue is sometimes called the "desert color of the sea."

≋ *What are algae?*

Most of the ocean's plants are algae. Some of these are microscopic, one-celled organisms, but others, such as the kelps, often grow to several hundred feet in length.

Algae do not require true roots, stems, or leaves, as they can absorb water and nutrients from their environment. However, some algae have what is termed a *holdfast*, a structure that holds the plant in place. This holdfast is not a root because it does not absorb water and nutrients from the soil. In addition, some algae have blades like leaves, which are extensions of the plant body. The function of these blades is to increase the surface area of the

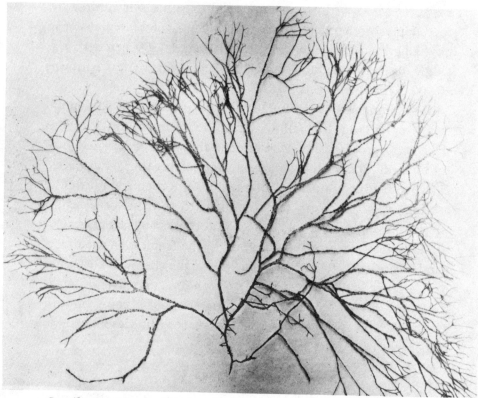

Gracilaria folifera—a species of marine algae. *(Courtesy NOAA)*

plant body itself and to facilitate absorption and photosynthesis (the synthesized formation of carbohydrates, proteins, and fats, plus carbon dioxide and other organic compounds, by action of the sun's rays on chlorophyll).

What is the place of algae in the ocean's food chain?

The term *food chain* means the passing of nutrients from one animal or plant to another, progressing from the simplest to the most complex organisms. The food chain begins with the microscopic algae, which billions of minute, floating animals and

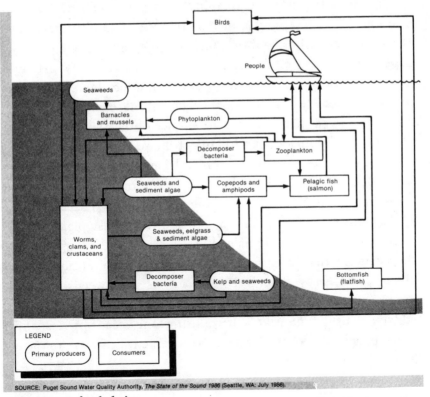

SOURCE: Puget Sound Water Quality Authority, *The State of the Sound 1986* (Seattle, WA: July 1986).

The ocean's food chain.

plants—known as plankton—eat to build their bodies. Then the younger fish, plankton-feeding fishes (such as the menhaden and herrings), crustaceans (such as crabs, lobsters, and shrimp), and many other sea animals feed on the plankton. They, in turn, are eaten by larger carnivores as tuna, halibut, shark, and squid. When these animals die, the nutrients return to the ocean to be used by succeeding generations.

What are seaweeds?

Other kinds of marine algae are commonly called *seaweeds*, a highly useful group of plants that yield a number of products having many important uses. The larger plants can be divided into four classes: (1) green, or *chlorophyceae*; (2) blue-green, or *cyanophyceae*; (3) brown, or *phaeophyceae*; and (4) red, or *rhodophyceae*. These algae are found in saltwater. They usually grow not in the open ocean but in the high intertidal regions and in clear waters less than 300 feet deep; one exception is the sargassum weed that floats on the surface of the Sargasso Sea.

Because the major constituents of the seaweeds are carbohydrates, as well as protein, fat, minerals, and vitamins, seaweeds have been used as feed for domesticated animals (especially in areas around the North Sea), and they have also been used as food for humans (particularly in Asia). In addition, these plants were considered to have medicinal value as far back as 3000 B.C.. Both the Japanese and Chinese used them to treat goiter and other glandular diseases. The early Romans used seaweeds to heal burns, rashes, and wounds; the British often ate Porphyra (an edible red alga) to prevent scurvy during long ocean voyages; and other peoples have used seaweeds to remedy various stomach and intestinal disorders.

The seaweeds along the coasts are among the oceans' most valuable living resources. The greatest value of seaweeds in

Seaweed. *(Courtesy NOAA)*

America has come from the chemical and industrial products derived from them. These products—for example, algin, agar, and carrageenin—can be used in foods, such as ice cream, candies, and cake icings; in drugs, such as aspirin and antacid tablets and calamine lotions; and in manufacturing processes producing rubber, textiles, acoustic tiles, and numerous other commercial items. Another derivative of seaweeds, mannitol, is used in explosives and medicinal drugs.

How many different species of ocean fish are there?

The total number of species of ocean fish ranges from 15,000 to over 40,000, with the figure of 25,000 most often cited. There are several reasons for the discrepancy. Some fish species have not yet been named, and others are often named more than once because of inadequate descriptions and variations in geographical distribution. Also, it sometimes is difficult to distinguish between the male and female of the same species because of striking differences in their body configurations and color patterns. Confusion over this sexual *dimorphism*, as it is termed, has often caused the male to be designated as belonging to one species and the female to another. For example, some 400 species of grouper fish are noted for their sensational colors and ability to change colors. More than this, however, they mature first as females and a few years later change into males. Different kinds of groupers change at different ages (from 7 to 10 years), and the larger sizes of all species are males.

Life in saltwater in some ways is not as rigorous as is life in freshwater. Temperature variations in the ocean are smaller than those in freshwater, and any fluctuations are gradual. Saltwater also circulates an abundance of substances necessary for life. All these factors combine to make the ocean environment especially favorable for fish and a wide variety of other living forms.

What are the differences between bony and cartilaginous fish?

There are two main classes of ocean fish living today, the Ostreichthyes, or bony fish, and the Chondrichthyes, or cartilaginous fish. Most bony fish, or those with a skeleton of bone, have slim, streamlined, oval-shaped bodies normally covered in scales and equipped with seven or more fins. Their gills have a cover called a *operculum*. Bony fish also have a swim bladder, a balloonlike bag filled with gas (including oxygen) that helps keep them afloat. Cod, sailfish, salmon, eels, and tuna are examples of bony fish, a class that numbers perhaps more than 25,000 species.

The cartilaginous fish, represented by some 600 species of sharks and rays, have a skeleton of cartilage—the same flexible substance found in the nose and ears of humans. These fish have wider and flatter bodies than do bony fish. Their bodies do not have scales but are covered by a rough surface skin. They have five gill slots, and essentially the same fin pattern as do bony

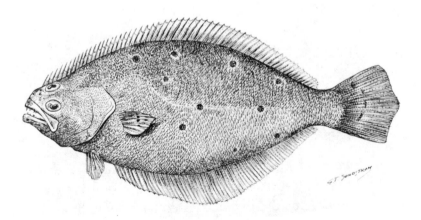

A bony fish, the summer flounder. *(Courtesy NOAA)*

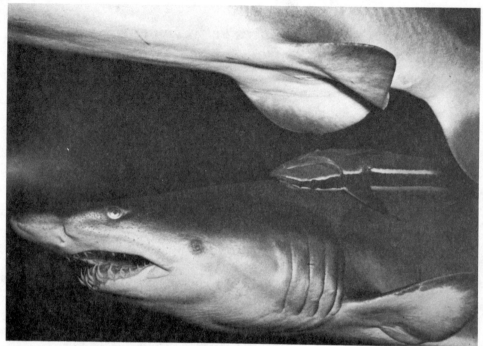

A cartilaginous fish, the sand tiger shark (with remora, or shark sucker). *(Courtesy U.S. Fish and Wildlife Service)*

fish, although their tail fin is different. Unlike bony fish, cartilaginous fish do not have a swim bladder, and therefore they must never stop swimming, for otherwise they would drown.

Can fish be part bony and part cartilaginous?

The two classes of living ocean fish each have several distinctly different features, and so their separation is generally rather arbitrary. But the two classes do have some links, and a few fish exhibit features of both bony fish and cartilaginous fish.

A coelacanth. *(Courtesy U.S. Fish and Wildlife Service)*

One such a fish is the *coelacanth*. The first indication that it existed came in 1938, when one was netted off the east coast of Africa. This hitherto unseen fish was taken to a biologist who identified it. Its discovery astounded scientists everywhere at the time and was hailed as the most important natural history discovery of the century. In the past few years several more coelacanth have been caught. In 1987, a team of West German scientists in a small submarine observed six coelacanths in depths from 380 to 600 feet in the western Indian Ocean near the Comoros Islands. The coelacanth has fins attached to a scaly stalk that protrudes from its cigar-shaped body. Such a feature seems to indicate that during its evolution one of its ancestors might have become an amphibian, a vertebrate animal adapted to live both in the water and on land.

Are all fish "cold blooded?" And how do they breathe?

With the exception of certain tunas and bonitos, most marine fishes are cold blooded. This means that their body temperature is about the same as that of the surrounding water. To breathe, fish take in this water by opening and closing their mouth. In this way they absorb the oxygen in the water into their gills from which it passes into their blood. The carbon dioxide then passes out of their blood into the water and is washed away.

How long do fish and other marine animals live?

No one yet knows, but it is thought that most fishes never live more than 25 years. For example, the tarpon's life span is about 16 years maximum; the Atlantic cod and herring around 22; the haddock 15; the bluefin tuna 13; the great barracuda about 15; and the spiny dogfish, an exception, up to 30 years. There is no reliable way to determine a fish's age; however, the shells of some animals such as clams and scallops have rings like those of trees, which have yearly divisions. Sea scallops' rings indicate that they may live as long as 16 years.

In what parts of the ocean do most fish live?

Marine fish, like all other animals, show a preference for certain geographic regions. Most marine fish live in either the *littoral zone*, or the region along the coasts, including the waters

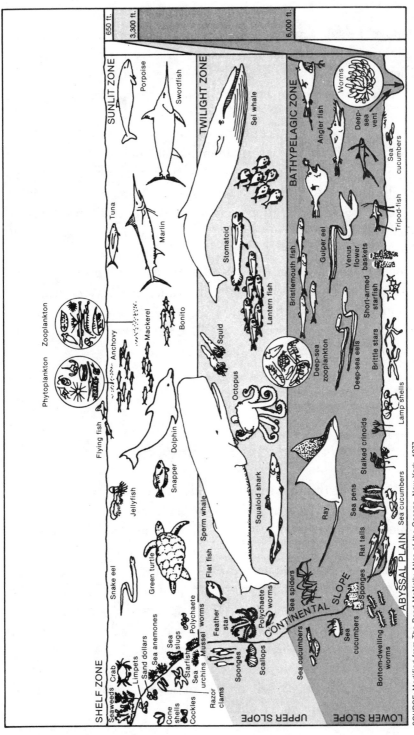

SOURCE: Modified from The Rand McNally Atlas of the Oceans, New York, 1977.

The distribution of marine life in the sea.

above the submerged land of the continental shelves to a depth of 400 to 600 feet, or the *pelagic zone,* or the open ocean waters, to depths of about 4000 to 6000 feet. Relatively few in number and species of the bony and cartilaginous fishes live in depths of 18,000 feet.

The littoral zone contains, by far, the widest variety of fish. Some are bottom dwellers (demersals), such as cod, sole, and flounder. Others live in the shallow waters along the coast, and still others swim farther out into the open ocean. The continental shelves are home to more than two-thirds of all the species of fish (about 17,000 species). Most of these fish live within 20 miles of the shore. Some fish, such as salmon and shad, spend most of their lives in the ocean but return to their birth streams and rivers to spawn. Fish, like the tuna, marlin, and mackerel, wander widely in the open ocean, favoring areas in the upper layers but no deeper than about 3000 feet, that is, in those layers whose temperature they find comfortable.

What is the deep scattering layer?

Most of the fish that live at depths of 650 to 2600 feet are small exotic fish that have swim bladders. Gas bubbles in the bladder reflect sound waves, which led scientists in the 1940s to discover that fish live in layers in the ocean that moved to the surface at sunset and descended at sunrise. This mid-depth stratum is known as a *deep scattering layer,* as it reflects or scatters echo-ranging sonar pulses. This movement is caused by the nightly migrations of fish such as hatchetfish (about three inches long), lanternfish, bristlemouths, and bigscales. With some exceptions, the fish in these four families have reflective swim bladders, and most fish in the mid-ocean depths have light-producing organs called *photophores.*

How deep have fish been found?

Until the HMS *Challenger* expedition (1872–1876), most people believed that no animals could exist in water much lower than about 2000 feet. The pressure at this depth is approximately 900 pounds per square inch, which, it was believed, would crush all life. However, the *Challenger* netted many creatures from these depths, and since that time we have learned much about the bizarre and fascinating forms of life that inhabit the deepest depths of the ocean. For example, in 1951, the Danish ship *Galathea* caught thousands of animals—fish, clams, worms, starfish—living at 7000-to 25,000-foot depths. Many also were found on the ocean floor, 33,431 feet deep. Three fish among the many brought up from other great depths were a typhlonus, a blind fish with a mouth shaped like a shovel (caught at 16,798 feet in the Celebes Sea); a fish named Galatheathauma axeli, which has a large luminous organ in its mouth (caught at 10,880 feet in the Pacific off Central America); and the Bassogigas, caught at 23,530 feet.

How many kinds of ocean birds are there?

Of the approximate 8000 different species of all birds, a relatively small number are classified as ocean birds or birds that live on and over the ocean during a major portion of their lives, such as albatrosses, shearwaters, fulmars, and petrels. These migratory birds are equipped with a salt gland that excretes excess salt to prevent dehydration, and their bodies are especially designed for flying for long periods rather than for walking on land. Shorebirds, those that live around the ocean shores, such as gulls, sandpipers, and penguins, do not have the same characteristics that the true ocean birds have.

Fulmars. *(Courtesy U.S. Fish and Wildlife Service)*

Ocean birds like puffins, fulmars, and petrels cross the Atlantic from Europe to North America, and the Arctic skua and the Atlantic cormorant fly from northern Europe to the African coasts. But, the most impressive long-distance flyers are the Arctic tern and the albatross. The Arctic tern, which is the size of a small sea gull, regularly migrates from its breeding ground in the Arctic to the Antarctic. Then it molts in the Antarctic and returns to the Arctic to nest each year. The albatross lives on and around the ocean and flies around the world, especially during its first few years of life.

Is coral an animal?

Coral is a carnivorous animal closely related to the jellyfish. There are many species and four main types: solitary, colonial, hard, and soft. As these names imply, the solitary corals exist as

Coral. *(Courtesy U.S. Navy)*

individual organisms, and the colonial type is a colony of individual corals. The hard corals have hard skeletons of calcium carbonate (limestone). They grow in a variety of colors (red, purple, orange, and yellow) and forms, including branching corals, mushroom corals, massive corals, brain-shaped corals, and staghorn corals. Soft corals do not have calcareous skeletons, like the hard corals but they do have the ability to move, and they take advantage of this to fight off the hard corals by approaching them and releasing toxic chemicals. These chemicals accumulate in the hard corals' tissues, retarding their growth and eventually killing them.

 ## How do coral reefs form?

After the coral completes its larva stage, it forms a polyp, a single organism consisting of a soft, tubular body closed at the bottom with a mouth and surrounded by venomous tentacles at the top. The center of the tube is the coral's stomach.

In order to develop and grow, the coral must anchor itself to something, either the ocean bottom or a rocky surface. A congregation of such anchored corals thus forms a reef. The coral feeds by snaring, with its paralyzing tentacles, tiny floating organisms (plankton).

The living coral reefs—such as those in the Caribbean, the Great Barrier Reef of Australia (the largest coral formation in the world)—are made up of hard corals. The corals in the colony are connected by extensions of their tissues, even those of their stomach cavities. As the colony grows, it is slowly cemented into stony mass, with new skeletons laid down over old. Over the centuries, this mass gradually expands, with the living coral occupying only its surface. With a favorable water temperature (82°–85°F), salinity (27–28 ppt), and adequate nutrients, coral reefs can grow about one inch per year. Storm waves, boring marine worms, and various predators such as the crown of thorns starfish all help limit such growth.

Scientists have developed a method of determining coral growth rates based on living coral's assimilation of radium isotopes. When the coral forms its skeleton of calcium carbonate, the radium isotopes decay at known rates; thus, samples collected through a massive coral growth (called a *head*) may be dated to determine how fast the coral is growing. The banding and radium methods may be used to review changes in growth rate as the coral adapts to changes in the environment in which it is growing. Data from corals also may be used to reconstruct patterns of radioactive fallout and to monitor changes in local water chemistry.

Are some ocean shells poisonous?

Some rather innocent and beautifully marked seashells, including one of the most valuable of all to collectors—the glory of the seas *(Conus gloria-maris)*—can be very dangerous to humans. Most of the 500 species of cone shells—which, as the name suggests, are shaped like a truncated cone—contain a marine snail. This snail is equipped with a potent venom and a hair trigger dart appartus that can kill fish, worms, and even humans who handle the shell. Some of the most dangerous of the tropical species, which may be buried in the sand or under rocks and near coral are the court cone and the marbled cone, which can be found from Polynesia to the Indian Ocean; the striated cone, which inhabits the area from Australia to East Africa; and the textile and tulip cones, which range from Polynesia to the Red Sea.

Are all sharks dangerous?

The most generally feared fish are sharks. Their bad reputation is understandable, as injuries from shark bites are usually severe and frequently fatal. Yet, there have been fewer than 750 shark attacks on people reported in the past 400 years.

About 27 species of the more than 250 known species of sharks have been implicated in attacks on humans. However, all sharks over three feet long, or any large animal equipped with sharp teeth, may be dangerous and should be left alone. In short, although most sharks are harmless, they are unpredictable and may bite swimmers who bother them.

The kinds of sharks that are known to have attacked humans without apparent provocation include the gray shark, white-tip shark, blue shark, tiger shark, the mako, white shark, and the hammerhead. Except for the hammerheads, whose name indicates their appearance, all the other sharks look pretty much alike to the untrained eye. Very few people who swim in the ocean can spot a shark's pedigree with enough accuracy to determine friend or foe. The best procedures, therefore, is not to panic if you see a shark but to leave the water as quickly and quietly as possible. It is also prudent not to swim in areas where sharks are known to be present, in turbid water, or in water where refuse has been discarded. Don't wear bright, shining objects while swimming, as such objects may attract the attention not only of sharks but also of barracudas.

Are barracudas dangerous?

There are some 20 species of barracuda, and those that reach a length of four or more feet may be a hazard to swimmers. However, although these fish have the unnerving habit of follow-

A great barracuda. *(Courtesy NOAA)*

ing divers, they do not often attack them. When barracudas do attack, it is usually in murky water, where visibility is limited, and the fish probably sees only a moving hand or foot, which may appear as prey.

Barracudas such as the great barracuda, *sphyraena barracuda*, may grow to six to eight feet in length and are found in the West Indies and Brazil, north to Florida, and in the Indo-Pacific from the Hawaiian Islands to the Red Sea. Other species include the Northern barracuda of the western North Atlantic; the European barracuda of the Mediterranean and eastern Atlantic; the Indian barracuda and Commerson's barracuda, both of the Indian Ocean; and the California barracuda.

What about moray eels?

Like barracudas, moray eels have a far worse reputation than they deserve. There are 120 species of moray eels, with a few living in the warmer temperate regions of California and Europe. They range in size from six inches to 10 feet or more long, with an ugly, snakelike appearance. Most morays try to avoid any contact with humans, just as most humans try to avoid them. Those swimmers and divers who have been injured by morays have usually been hurt when they put their hands into rock crevices searching for lobsters or crabs. The moray, perhaps feeling threatened or mistaking the hand for prey, then has struck out and bitten. They can cause severe wounds in this way as well as when they are cornered or speared.

A moray eel. *(Courtesy U.S. Fish and Wildlife Service)*

Besides biting, how else can fish sometimes be dangerous to people?

Especially in the warmer ocean waters there are some types of venomous fish. Their sting is usually on their fin spines or those somewhere on their bodies. Stingrays, for example, have one or more spearlike spines near the base of a tail that can whip around to inflict venomous wounds that can be fatal. The 100 species of stingrays range in size from 1 to 15 feet across the fins, and they can weigh from 2 to 700 pounds. Living in tropical and temperate ocean waters worldwide, stingrays may be found along both coasts of the United States. Because they spend most of their time on the bottom in shallow waters, if a swimmer enters these waters with a shuffling gait, he or she will usually cause the fish to move on and out of the way. Stepping down on one can lead to rather painful results.

Other ocean fish, such as scorpionfishes and stonefishes, are also capable of inflicting wounds. The 300 species of scorpion-fishes live mainly in temperate ocean waters, although a few are found in the tropics. Those that live in shallow water are the most venomous, and because they lie on the bottom of these areas, they can be quite difficult to see. Most of the scorpion-fishes give a painful wound, but no more. But the stonefishes, which on the ocean bottom are very difficult to distinguish from a rock, can inflict a fatal wound to the swimmer who steps down on one. The 3 species of stonefish are found from the Red Sea to East Africa and across the Indian Ocean to the northern coasts of Western Australia and Queensland.

Surgeonfishes are so named because they possess spines (lancets) that can cut flesh as cleanly as can a surgeon's scalpel. Some 200 species are found from Madagascar across the Indo-Pacific to Hawaii. They grow to two feet in length, are venomous, and the wounds they can inflict by the spines on their fins are much like those produced by the scorpionfishes.

One of the most troublesome marine animals to swimmers is the sea urchin. Those that live on tropical reefs belong to a class called *echinoderms* (which also includes the starfishes), which are known to be venomous. Those that live in temperate waters are not venomous. Sea urchins average in size to about two to three inches measured across their round, hard, spiny skeleton. Any accidental contact with the animal's spines, whether or not they contain venom, can cause a painful injury.

Some corals sting as well, but more serious is that they can cut when they are touched or rubbed by a swimmer. Since a swimmer's skin has been softened by the water, the many sharp edges and abrasive surfaces that are present on the bottom of the ocean, such as those of barnacles and corals, pose a hazard for the unattentive swimmer.

Sea urchins. *(Courtesy NOAA)*

What are jellyfishes?

Certain organisms found floating on water throughout the oceans (and even in freshwater) have probably caused more inconvenience and pain to swimmers than all of the other ocean

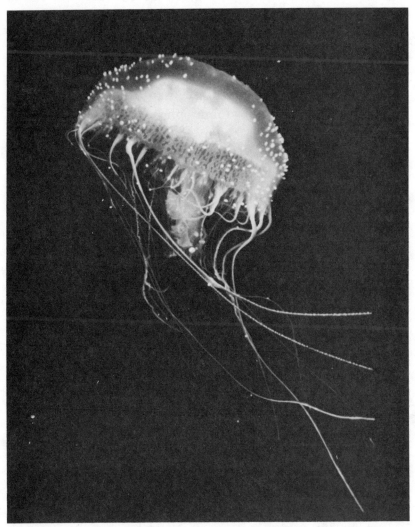

A jellyfish.

animals combined. These culprits are the jellyfishes and their relatives. Jellyfishes belong to a division of the animal kingdom (coelenterata) that includes the corals and several other species, such as sea fans and anemones. All of them have generally the same design: a central cavity with an opening surrounded by stinging tentacles. On jellyfish, these tentacles can sting if touched. The strength of their poison varies from harmless to painful to fatal. For example, the box jellyfish accounts for an average of three deaths a year in the ocean waters around Australia. The box jellyfish, so named because of its cubical body, is the world's only jellyfish known to be lethal to humans.

The well-known Portuguese man-of-war looks like a jellyfish, although, as a siphonophore, it differs from the jellyfishes in that it is a colony of separate parts, with each having a specialized function, like swimming or catching food. Attached to its gas-filled float are several trailing tentacles, some as long as 30 feet. Each tentacle, armed with *nematocycsts*, can inflict a very painful sting on swimmers who touch them.

 ## What are skates?

There are some 100 species of marine animals called *skates*. All these fish have broad, flat bodies with winglike fins and a slender tail with two small dorsal fins. The skates are related to sharks and also to rays, with which they are often confused, as they both have similar shapes.

Skates are found mostly in shallow temperate and tropical waters in all the world's oceans except for the South Pacific, and a portion of the northeast coast of Latin America. One common skate, *Raja batis*, attains a length of over 6 feet, and when young, it lives on a diet of various bottom-living animals (such as crabs and lobsters). Later, they also eat other fish (especially herring) which they hunt mainly by scent rather than by sight. Most skate species live on or near the bottom in shallow waters. However, some are found at 600-foot depths, and one species, the deep-sea skate *(Raja abyssicola)*, lives over a mile deep in the Pacific Ocean off the coast of North America. All skates are good swimmers when the occasion demands, and all, when lying on the bottom, breathe with their mouths closed so as not to swallow mud or sand. Water is taken in through passages in the top of the head and passes out through gill slits on the fish's underside. The eyes are on top of a diamond-shaped body. The male has small pelvic fins equipped with a pair of claspers or organism for injecting sperm into the female. The female's eggs are contained in a fiber-reinforced case called a *mermaid's purse.*

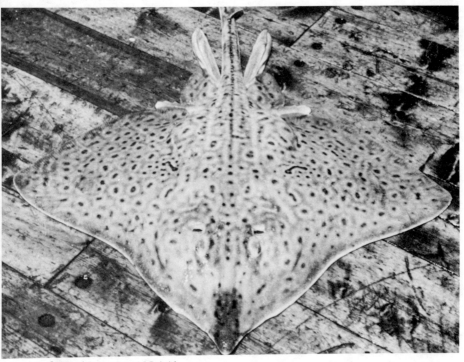

A skate. *(Courtesy NOAA)*

What are octopuses?

Octopuses are mollusks and also are relatives of the squid and cuttlefish. They have a baglike body and eight tapered arms, or tentacles, each of which has a double row of suckers running down it. Octopuses can change color at will, to make themselves less visible to their enemies. If this camouflage does not work, they will squirt an inky fluid in the face of their pursuer. Octopuses also are famous escape artists, needing only a space as big as their neck to make an exit.

An octopus. *(U.S. Fish and Wildlife Service)*

What are squid?

Squid are among the most abundant of marine animals and are found in ocean waters throughout the world, usually in waters over the continental shelves from the coastline to the shelf edge. Squid have an internal shell and 10 tentacles. One pair protrudes and has suckers at the ends, whereas the other shorter four pairs have suckers over their entire length.

Squid, like the octopus, also have an ink sac and chromatophores that provide protective coloration. Most of the

A cuttlefish. *(Courtesy NOAA)*

smaller species of squid range between four and eight inches in length. They feed on small fish, crustaceans, and other marine organisms. In turn, they furnish food for the *pinnipeds* (seals, sea lions, and walruses), large fish, whales, and sea birds. Squid are highly valued as food in many parts of the world. In addition, because of their highly developed sensor organs and nervous systems, squid are of great interest to scientists. For example, the squid's eye is used to determine certain aspects of photoreception—or how the pigments in the eye's cells affect vision. The squid's giant nerve fiber also contributes to our knowledge of nerve conduction.

An interesting relative of the squid is the cuttlefish. Unlike shrimp and crab, whose skeletons are external, the cuttlefish's is internal. This skeleton is called a *cuttlebone;* it can be ground to a powder and used in dentifrices and polishes. When trying to escape an enemy, the cuttlefish throws out a dense brownish cloud. This "ink" is known as *sepia* and was once used in watercolor painting and in photography.

What are krill?

Krill are shrimplike creatures about an inch in length and are the main food of the whalebone whales in the Antarctic. This animal plankton, *Euphausia superba,* occurs in vast numbers in this region, with some estimates at about 1 billion tons per year.

What is the difference between dolphins and porpoises?

The term *dolphin* and *porpoise* are often used interchangeably, but there are some differences between these two warm-

A bottle nose dolphin. *(Courtesy U.S. Navy)*

blooded, air-breathing mammals. The dolphin is a sharp-toothed whale with a prominent beak or snout and a somewhat curved dorsal (back) fin. The porpoise, on the other hand, is a smaller whale with spade-shaped teeth, no beak, and a triangular dorsal fin. Porpoises are usually under 6 feet in length, whereas dolphins range in size from 7 to 12 feet.

The most well known dolphin, and the one most frequently seen performing in marine exhibitions, is the Atlantic bottle nose dolphin. This friendly animal is commonly referred to as a "porpoise," but it actually is not. Another dolphin, the saddleback, lives in both the Pacific and Atlantic oceans. Its distinctive markings include a saddlelike pattern of dark color on the back, as well as a dark ring around each eye. It generally does not grow over 7 feet long. It lives in the open ocean and often accompanies oceangoing vessels.

A true porpoise, the harbor porpoise, reaches a length of no more than six feet. Its back is gray to black, and its underside is grayish white to pure white. It is one of the best known and most representative of the few species of porpoises in the Phocaenidae family, as opposed to the some 33 species of Cetacean mammals called dolphins that belong to the Delphinidae family.

Are some dolphins also whales?

Some members of the Delphinidae family grow so large that they are called whales rather than dolphins. The largest of these is the killer whale, which grows to a length of 30 feet. It is black with sharply contrasting areas of white or yellow, with an extremely large dorsal (back) fin in the adult whales. This Cetacean is found only in cold ocean waters.

Another large whale of the same family is the pilot whale, which reaches a length of 20 feet or more. Pilot whales have big round heads and are almost solid black. Killer whales and pilot whales in captivity have proved to be gentle, good natured, and quick to learn. All of these warm-blooded, air-breathing mammals are remarkable animals. Dolphins are the only wild creatures that as adults, will actually seek out human company and attempt to engage them in play.

Where do the whales often seen off California come from?

California gray whales migrate along the Pacific coast of the United States around the first of the year. They leave the icy waters of the Sea of Okhotsk (one of the marginal seas on the northern rim of the Pacific Ocean) to reach Seammons Lagoon and Magdalena Bay to breed in the spring in the warm shallow waters off Baja California. No other large whales migrate so regularly or are so acclimated to coastal waters.

What is bioluminescence?

Bioluminescence, the emission of visible light by living organisms, is a characteristic of many near-surface ocean creatures. However, it is in the deepest parts of the ocean that bioluminescence has reached a high state of development, with more than two-thirds of the species producing light. Some fishes, squids, and euphausiids (krill) possess "searchlights" with lens, reflectors, and irises almost as complex as those of the human eye.

THE GEOLOGICAL OCEAN

4

Hast Thou entered into the springs of the sea,
or hast Thou walked in search of the depth?

Hast Thou perceived the breadth of the earth?
Declare if Thou knowest it all.

Job 38:16, 18

How is geology used in oceanography?

Geology is concerned with the physical nature and history of
the earth, including the structure and development of its surface,
the composition of its interior, rock types, and the forms of life
found as fossils. Geology has three main branches: mineralogy
and petrology, the study of the classification, location, composition, and structure of minerals and rocks; physical geology, the
processes that bring about changes in the earth; and historical
geology, the history of these changes. Stratigraphy is that part of
historical geology concerned with the description, organization,
and classification of stratified rocks. Paleontology, also a part of
historical geology, is the study of the fossilized remains of the
ancestral plants and animals that inhabited the earth in ancient

times. Marine geology is the study of the geological processes responsible for the origin, shape, structure, properties, and history of the ocean floor, including its sediment and rocks.

What have geologists learned about the planet's ocean?

Geologists have learned that all the continents are surrounded by gently sloping platforms of varying widths, the continental shelves. Descending abruptly from the shelves are the continental slopes, which end in the great ocean basins. The bottom of the ocean is not a level plain but is marked by mountains and valleys. Indeed, the world's largest mountain range is in the Atlantic Ocean, and its tallest peak, 27,000 feet high, forms an island in the Azores. The ocean floor also contains great depressions, or trenches, the deepest one probably being the Mindanao Trench off the Philippines, with its bottom about six and a half miles below the surface.

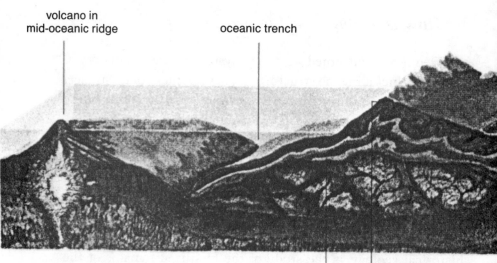

volcano in
mid-oceanic ridge oceanic trench

upper granitic crust

The ocean floor.

lower granitic crust

Geologists have also learned that the floor of the Pacific is underlaid with basalt, a tough, fine-grained-to-dense volcanic rock, whereas other ocean floors are made of granite. The ocean floor itself holds enormous amounts of minerals. For instance, manganese nodules on the ocean floor range in size from a fraction of a pound up to nearly a ton. Besides the nodules, the ocean floor is covered with about 40 million square miles of red clay (not generally in the same areas as the nodules). This clay is on the abyssal plains in very deep water and contains about 50 percent silica, 20 percent aluminum, 12 percent iron oxide, and smaller amounts of manganese, nickel, cobalt, copper and vanadium.

Petroleum also originated in the ocean, both along its edges where once-submerged lands have risen as in the Middle East and in the Gulf of Mexico, or in areas once covered by ancient inland seas, as in Oklahoma. In recent years, geologists have tapped the continental shelves, seeking oil deposits beneath the ocean floor. As a result, offshore wells are producing oil today off the coasts of Texas and Louisiana in the Gulf of Mexico, and off California in the Pacific.

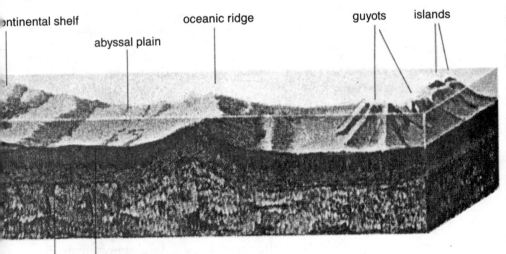

continental shelf   oceanic ridge   guyots   islands

abyssal plain

basaltic crust

mantle

In addition, the ocean waters hold about 50 quadrillion tons of dissolved mineral salts which have been accumulating for a billion years or more. Ash from volcanoes sifting into the rivers is carried to the ocean, bringing with it chlorine and sulphur. Soil-laden waters also carry calcium and silicon to the ocean, from weathering rock and eroding land.

▨ What is the earth's crust?

Sometime after the earth was formed, about 4.5 billion years ago, its components separated into three concentric units: the crust, mantle, and core.

The crust is the earth's outer shell layer that underlies all the oceans, other surface waters, and land features. It represents only three- to four-tenths of 1 percent of the planet's total mass and is the only portion that has been extensively sampled and chemically analyzed. Its thickness varies from about 3 to 6 miles under the oceans and from 15 to 22 miles beneath the continents but extends down to 30 miles under some mountain chains.

Below the crust is the mantle, a massive shell composed of dense, fine-grained rocks. The thickness of the mantle is a little less than half (1800+ miles) that of the earth's radius (3964 miles at the equator).

In the center of the earth is the core, a dense molten sphere slightly thicker than the mantle. Its volume is about one-eighth of that of the entire earth. Although the core's exact content is not known, it is thought to be molten iron.

The solid earth's "crusty" surface is composed of two main parts, or as the geologists would say, two physiographic provinces: the continents and the deep-ocean basins. There are fundamental geological differences between these provinces. For instance, the crust forming the continents is richer in silica

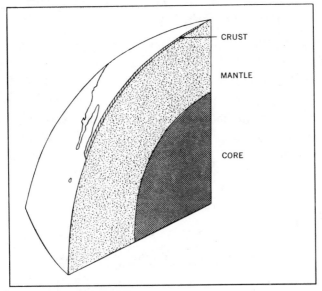

The layers of the earth.

(silicon dioxide, or hard, glassy minerals such as quartz and sand) and alkalis (mineral salts such as sodium and potassium), but poorer in iron and magnesium than is the oceanic crust. Also, the continental crust is about four times thicker than the oceanic crust but is only half as efficient in conducting heat.

What causes earthquakes?

Largely from research carried out on the ocean floor, it is known that the earth's crust is broken up into seven very large shell-like plates and a dozen or more smaller plates. It is generally believed that these so-called tectonic plates, which are in constant movement with respect to one another, are driven by (convective) motions in the underlying mantle. Such motions are powered by heat from the decay of radioactive elements, and so the crustal plates slide over a partially molten surface. These movements can produce earthquakes, volcanoes, and other changes on the earth's surface. For example, it has been estimated that the plate under the Pacific Ocean off Central America is moving at a rate of about four inches a year. This movement over the past several million years has been responsible for the land features of Costa Rica's Osa peninsula, which will be changed in the next million years or so by the plate's continuing movements.

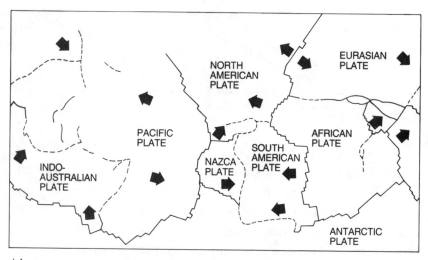

(a)

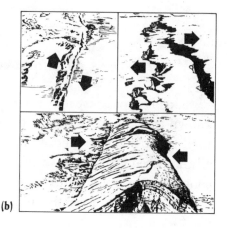

The earth's tectonic plates:
(a) crustal plate boundaries and
(b) relative plate motions
at boundaries.

(b)

The plates move in any one of three ways: They can pull away from one another, slide past one another, or converge. When the plates are pulled apart, the crack formed between them fills with hot material rising from the earth's center. This is added to the plates and as the cracking continues, more new material is added. Although the plates move only a few inches per year, the process, occurring over millions of years, forms oceanic ridges, such as the Mid-Atlantic ridge, a nearly continuous system of mountains over 59,000 miles long bisecting the Atlantic Ocean basin. In some places, where the plates collide, old crust is forced downward beneath another plate. These areas are marked by deep ocean trenches. The collisions of adjacent plates cause volcanoes, tsunamis, and earthquakes. The highest percentage of the total seismic energy released in earthquakes is distributed along the "ring of fire" that marks the boundary of the Pacific plate.

How are oceanic hot springs formed?

In some places, ocean water seeping down through cracks in the ocean floor circulates around the hot rocks in the lower crust and upper mantle. Metals in the rocks are dissolved and carried by the circulating water back up through the floor into metal-rich hot springs.

In 1987, a team of oceanographers in the submersible *Alvin* discovered in the Pacific a hydrothermal spring where they witnessed sulfide-ore deposits being emitted. It is believed that these deposits contain concentrations of iron, nickel, silver, and copper. Also clustered around some of these vents are still little understood life forms: bacteria nourished by the poisonous hydrogen sulfide, 10-foot-long-tube worms, and giant clams.

Other hot springs have been found on the floor of the Atlantic. These are of special research interest to scientists, as it is thought that these springs may differ in their venting process from others previously investigated, in which the water had not penetrated as deep in the crack and been exposed to the hot lower-crust and upper-mantle areas. The metals and the deposits formed in these latter springs thus would be different.

What does the ocean floor look like?

The most interesting part of the ocean is the bottom, which displays a wide variety of features, such as ridges, trenches, plains, and mountains formed by crustal deformation and volcanism. The Mid-Ocean ridge, the largest mountain range on earth, is so named because it has a mid-ocean position in all the oceans but the Pacific. In most places the ridges are flanked by hills and plains. These plains are essentially flat areas adjacent to the continental rises. Volcanoes are common on the ocean floor, and some form islands. *Guyots*—or flat-topped submarine mountains—and dormant volcanoes also can be seen. In the Pacific are deep trenches in areas associated with volcanic activity, and these lie near islands. The floor of the Pacific has been compared by oceanographers to the surface of the moon.

The ocean floor is divided into four areas: the continental shelf, the continental slope, the continental rise, and the deep ocean floor or basin. Collectively, the first three (shelf, slope, and rise) are called the *continental margin*, or the water-covered area from the shoreline of the continents to the deep ocean floor or basin.

The *continental shelf* is a zone that borders the continents. The area of the U.S. continental shelf is estimated to be approximately 1.6 million square nautical miles (1 square nautical mile equals 1.35 square statute miles). This shelf is a gently sloping water-covered surface area that extends outward and downward from the shoreline of the land to an ocean depth of 600 feet or

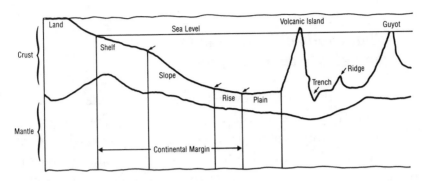

A profile of the ocean floor.

less, where the slope becomes abruptly steeper. The continental shelf varies in width from practically nothing to an average of 30 miles and up to 800 miles, the widest being off the Siberian Arctic coast. Contrary to what the name *shelf* implies, the continental shelves are not flat or uniform but often have numerous hills, terraces, and deep canyons.

The *continental slope* begins where the shelf terminates at water depths of 600 feet or less and where the slope becomes abruptly steeper. The slope width varies from 12 to 62 miles, and the slope usually ends at depths of 4900 to 11,000 feet in the ocean. The slopes appear to be composed of sediment (mud, 60 percent; sand, 25 percent; gravel and rocks, 10 percent; and shell fragments, 5 percent) derived largely from the shelf. Slightly more than 8 percent of the total ocean area (142 million square miles) is occupied by the slopes and 7 percent by the shelves.

The *continental rise* begins at the end of the slope. The rise is a gently sloping, wedge-shaped collection of sediment. Its width can range from zero—where long narrow depressions with steep sides called *trenches* exist—to some 370 miles. Sediments from the shelf and slope constitute much of the rise, which is cut in some places by submarine canyons that extend upward into the slope and shelf. Continental rises cover some 5 percent of the total ocean area.

What kinds of instruments are used in geological oceanography?

In 1870, the French novelist Jules Verne wrote in *Twenty Thousand Leagues Under the Sea*, "The great depths of the ocean are entirely unknown to us. Soundings cannot reach them." Verne was not a scientist, but he was correct. During his time the ocean proved an effective barrier to learning about the features below its surface. Even today, many details still remain unanswered, but scientists and engineers, armed with modern-day tools, have acquired some valuable information. They have probed, profiled, and studied the ocean's various depths and regional features, such as its bottom topography, sediment type, and mineral deposits as well as the movements of the massive shell-like plates that make up the earth's crust.

Sound has been one of the best tools used in geological oceanography. Echo soundings have been used for the past six decades to measure the depth of the ocean, which is the first order of business for the marine geologist. Before that time the "soundings" taken had nothing to do with sound. To take a "sounding"—an old nautical term meaning "to measure depth"— a weighted rope or wire line was reeled into the water, and when it reached bottom the amount of line reeled back in gave the depth measurement. In echo sounding, as in active sonar (the acronym for SOund Navigation And Ranging), sound waves are generated and transmitted through the ocean water. When they strike a submerged object, they are reflected back as echoes to a hydrophone or receiver where they are interpreted. Even the early crude sounders used in ocean geological research revealed some of the most spectacular features of the oceans—the continental shelves, the great trenches, and the mid-ocean ridges. Over the years, echo sounders have been greatly improved and now can make much more precise measurements.

The traditional method used by geological oceanographers to

A sonar device. *(Courtesy U.S. Navy)*

gather data about the ocean floor is *coring.* Cores are obtained by driving a metal tube into the bottom and then pulling up the tube by cable and removing and examining its contents. The ship *Glomar Challenger* was built especially for this purpose. In the late 1960s this ship with its special equipment enabled scientists to drill 300 holes and recover more than 12 miles of deep ocean cores. The various layers in these cores reveal useful information about geological history, such as the relative dates of volcanic eruptions and periods of glaciation.

Another method to obtain samples of bottom sediments and ocean rocks is to drag dredges along the bottom. Or a so-called

An orange-peel bottom sampler. *(Courtesy NOAA)*

A grab sampler. *(Courtesy U.S. Coast Guard)*

grab sampler can collect about 10 cubic feet of floor material. When a trip weight hits the ocean bottom, a camera installed on the device takes a photo of the bottom sediments and rocks; then the jaws of the sampler "grab" some of the floor material and snap shut.

The earth's gravity is the force that attracts bodies to it. Gravity measurements are used in geological studies to find gravity anomalies—the differences between observed and theoretical values—to help geologists locate mineral and oil deposits. Gravity measurements can be made by satellites, aircraft, and surface ships.

Magnetic-compass variation in all parts of the world was recognized early in the history of sailing as essential to safe

navigation. In 1492, Christopher Columbus noted compass variation by comparing it with the direction of the North Star. Today,
in order to find the true course of a ship or airplane, compass
courses must be corrected for magnetic variation. Because the
earth's magnetic field is constantly changing, continual survey
becomes necessary not only for improving ocean navigation but
also for studying the earth's geological history.

In summary, much of the equipment used today in geological
research is technologically sophisticated and requires advanced
electronic components and systems that are usually supported
by computers for recording and analysis.

Although computer-based equipment, which usually requires very accurate navigational capabilities (for example, seismic recorders or marine gravimeters), offers the most detailed
geological information, marine geological research and surveying
often still use less expensive tools, such as a research vessel
equipped with a good winch, a conventional echo sounder, a
bottom grab, a gravity or box corer, and a dredge. Both methods—
the advanced and the more simplified—contribute fundamental
knowledge leading to advances in mineral and energy resource
development, ocean engineering, mitigation of geological haz-
ards, and better maintenance of the environment.

What is in the sediment on the ocean floor?

The ocean floor itself is composed principally of soil and
rocks washed into the ocean by rivers, streams, winds, and
waves; the ash and lava from volcanos; and the remains of marine organisms. Within the ocean these inorganic and organic
materials are transported by ocean currents, winds, and ice.

Most of the ocean's sediments (such as sand, mud, and clay)
come from the land; therefore, the thickest deposits of sediments
are in waters near land. Because of this, the Atlantic Ocean has a

deposition rate of about twice that of the Pacific, as much of the Pacific is far from land.

The thickest deposits from the land are found on the relatively shallow continental margins, the areas that surround the major landmasses. In these sediment-rich shelf areas are particles of all sizes, from less than $1/400$ of an inch for mud grains to over 10 inches for rocks and boulders, and any size for coral. In general, the inorganic deposits near the shore are comparatively coarse (sand, gravel), whereas those in the deep ocean are much finer (clay). Different-sized materials may combine with one another. For example, mud may combine with sand or other types of materials. Sand is commonly found with gravel and rock. Gravel is common around coral, and both coral and shells are examples of organic material that is usually found in warm waters less than 600 feet deep, although their fragments may be carried to deeper areas by currents.

The deep-ocean floor, which has a fairly uniform depth of about 9000 to 13,000 feet throughout the world, contains clay but has relatively little sediment of land origin. Here, the process of sedimentation can be studied. The water circulation enriches certain top ocean layers so that biological production is unusually high. Microorganisms live and die in great numbers, and their remains fall slowly to the ocean floor to form carpets of sediment. This sediment, usually found in very deep water, is called an *ooze*—diatom or diamaceous ooze, radiolarian ooze, globigerina ooze, and pteropod ooze. The first two, diatom and radiolarian, come from the siliceous (containing silica) skeletons of plankton. The globigerina and pteropod oozes are made up of the calcareous (containing calcium and carbonate) remains of the *foraminifera* and *pteropod*, both of which are marine protozoans—one-celled microorganisms of the animal kingdom. All these remains are usually the sizes of mud and sand. The ecology of these sediments can reveal the earth's recent history.

Volcanoes also may form deposits on the ocean floor. For example, if the volcano forms an island, volcanic rock may be broken down by waves into particles of boulder, gravel, sand, mud sand, or mud (the ash spewed into the air by the volcano may settle on the ocean bottom as mud). These materials may be deposited either close to or far from their source.

What are manganese nodules, and where are they found in the ocean?

The element manganese, discovered in 1774, is required for the commercial production of all steels. No economical effective substitute has ever been found, and millions of tons of manganese ores are used each year to make steel. Manganese is needed also to produce aluminum and cast iron.

Several of the industrialized countries, including the United States, have no domestic reserves of manganese; therefore, they must import it from other countries, such as Brazil and the Republic of South Africa.

But scattered randomly about over large areas on the ocean floors of the Atlantic and Pacific are billions of tons of manganese deposits. These deposits are in the shape of small (usually one to six inches in diameter), dark brown, potato-shaped nodules containing an average of 25 to 35 percent manganese, 1 to 2 percent nickel, 1 to 2 percent copper, and 0.1 to 0.5 percent cobalt, among other minerals.

Ocean manganese nodules were first discovered when they were brought up from parts of the deep ocean floor during the famous oceanographic *Challenger* expedition of the 1870s. Later, in the early 1900s, Alexander Agassiz, on another research expedition, dredged up such nodules from many parts of the eastern Pacific Ocean. He concluded that they covered an area larger than that of the United States. During the International Geophysical Year (IGY) in 1957–1958, systematic studies were begun to determine the nodules' areas of occurrence, concentrations, depth in

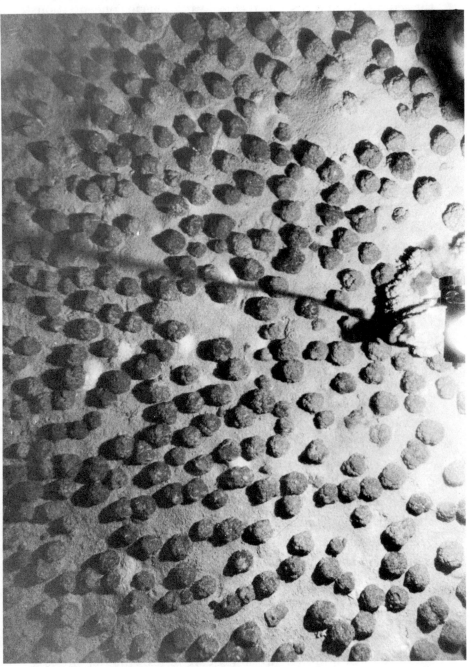

Manganese nodules. *(Courtesy Smithsonian Institution)*

the sediments, and possible regional variations in concentrations of contained metals. Since that time, these deposits have been extensively photographed on the ocean floor, and large quantities have been brought to the surface for chemical and other analyses.

Despite all this work, it is still somewhat of a scientific mystery as to how these manganese nodules are actually formed—whether by a purely inorganic process that takes place in the precipitation from ocean water or whether by bacterial action—how the nodules remain "afloat" on the sediment, how they capture manganese, and why they are older than the sediments.

There was no real commercial interest in these nodules as sources of metals until the late 1950s. Then, during the mid-1960s, several companies invested huge sums of money in ocean-floor exploration and nodule-recovery and -processing techniques. Although several preliminary mining systems for recovering the deposits have been sketched out since that time, little, if any, work has been done. As yet, not enough is known about the nature and extent of the deposits to allow the development of prototype mining systems. The investigations that have been made have been mainly to determine the economic value of the various nodule beds. Although the manganese nodules virtually litter the deep-ocean floors, they vary from location to location in size, quantities per unit area, and composition or quality. Most authorities have estimated that the average nodule concentration required for an economical mining operation is about 2.5 pounds per square foot, with dry weight compositions of 25 percent manganese, 1.5 percent nickel, about 1 percent copper, and about 0.3 percent cobalt. An area of some 20,000 square miles will probably be required to recover 3 million tons of these nodules per year for a period of 25 years.

The best areas for mining lie in the northeast equatorial Pacific Ocean between the Clarion and Clipperton fracture zones, an area of over 1 million square miles. Another site is a 300,000-square-mile area of the ocean southwest of Hawaii.

But such vast areas have not yet been adequately surveyed and mapped in regard to their geological features—submarine crevices, boulders, canyons, and cliffs—and such obstructions can make any mining operation extremely difficult if not impossible.

Thus, the physical character of the ocean terrain takes on a new significance, as the techniques studied and suggested for submarine mining range from vacuuming up the nodules to sliding them into sledlike collectors and loading them onto specifically configured ships. Such techniques have many problems, which require further research. Additional investigations are also needed regarding the best methods of recovering the various metals contained in the nodules.

Finally, besides the economic and technical questions yet to be resolved, there still are some international political obstacles to ocean mining operations, such as the legality of mining of various parts of the ocean.

What is the EEZ, and how will it affect work in the ocean?

The Exclusive Economic Zone (EEZ) is the area extending over a nation's adjacent territorial waters out to 200 nautical miles offshore. In the case of the United States, this means the addition of 2.9 billion acres to the 2.3 billion acres of dry land in the United States and its overseas possessions. More than 80 coastal nations have declared economic control over their EEZ. Accordingly, the United States can now legally exploit its EEZ for minerals such as cobalt, chromium, manganese, and platinum, all essential to peacetime and wartime metallurgy. But this capability depends on a better knowledge of the area's ocean floor than is now available. One measure of this limited capability is the number of U.S. personnel now involved in ocean work: The National Research Council estimated that more than 4000 U.S.

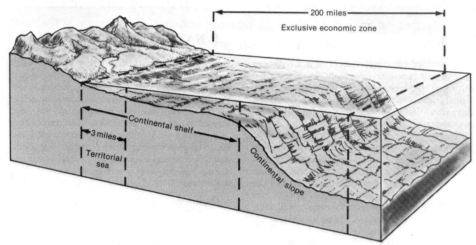

The EEZ, or Exclusive Economic Zone.

scientists are now working in ocean-related fields and that some 2700 U.S. oceanographers plus more than 56,000 people work in 12 federal agencies that administer a variety of oceanographic research programs, both inside and outside the EEZ.

What are some geological features of the Indian Ocean and the Persian Gulf?

Covering an area of about 32 million square miles, the Indian Ocean is the third largest of the world's oceans. Unlike the Atlantic and Pacific oceans, most of the Indian Ocean's waters flow south of the equator. The Indian Ocean was the first major ocean to serve as a trade route. In ancient days Arab sailors carried on a profitable trade among the ports of eastern Africa, the Persian Gulf, and the west coast of India. But not until the late fifteenth century was the Indian Ocean explored. In 1498,

Vasco de Gama began this era of exploration when he successfully rounded the Cape of Good Hope. This was followed by several more voyages, notably those of Sir Francis Drake in 1580, Abel Tasman in 1642, and James Cook in 1772–1776.

Still, until the middle of the twentieth century, oceanographers had little information about the Indian Ocean, and so it was known as the "forlorn ocean." But now this situation has changed, and we now know that the mean depth of the Indian Ocean is 14,055 feet and that it occupies a volume of some 84 million cubic miles. Its maximum depth, 24,442 feet, is just south of Java in the Java Trench, an area of active earthquake activity. These disturbances are caused by one of the earth's tectonic plates, the Indian plate, moving underneath the Eurasian plate. Also on the Indian Ocean floor is the Mid–Indian Ocean ridge—a system of ridges caused by the junction of three moving tectonic plates—the Antarctic, African, and Indian. Earthquakes are common in this area.

The Mid–Indian Ocean ridge divides the bed of the Indian Ocean into several basins, ranging from 162 to 4860 (nautical) miles in width. At the 10-thousand to 20-thousand-foot depths are smooth plains (among the flattest areas on the earth's crust) along with seamounts and hills.

The salt content (salinity) of most of the Indian Ocean's surface waters varies from 32 to 37 partial salinity units (psu) or 32 to 37 parts per thousand. Both salinity and temperature variations are generally greatest in the uppermost 3000-foot levels of the ocean; below this depth they do not vary appreciably. The waters of the Red Sea and Persian Gulf are the most salty because of high rates of evaporation, whereas the least salty waters are found in the Bay of Bengal (because of the high rainfall in that area) and the southern Indian Ocean (because of the thawing Antarctic ice pack).

The Persian Gulf, an arm of the Indian Ocean, is nearly surrounded by Iraq and Kuwait on the northwest; Saudi Arabia,

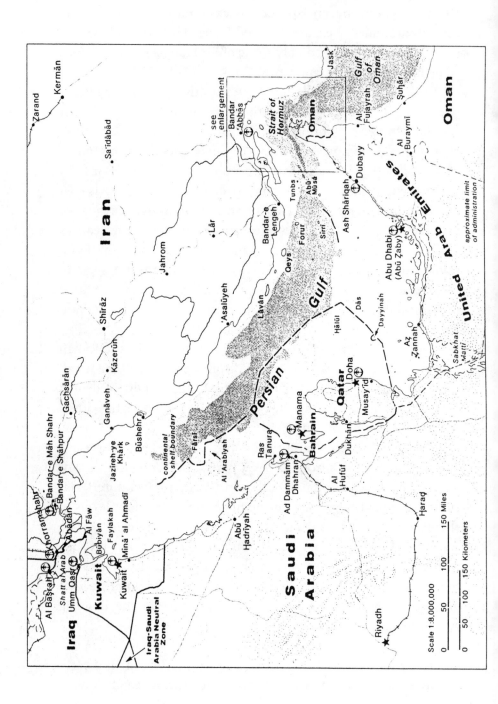

Qater, and Oman on the west and south; and Iran on the east.
The gulf is 615 miles long and 35 to 210 miles wide. It covers an
area of 93,026 square miles and has a volume of 2400 cubic
miles. Its mean depth is about 130 feet, although depths over 500
feet have been measured. Freshwater enters the gulf from only
one waterway, the Shatt al Arab, which receives the combined
flow of the Tigres, Euphrates, and Karun rivers. Even with this
flow, the gulf's waters would soon dry up through evaporation
were they not continually replenished by Indian Ocean water
moving through the Strait of Hormuz. Hundreds of islands dot
the gulf; its shoreline is fringed in many places by coral reefs,
sandbars, and mud flats; and the shallow water along its southern coast makes near-shore navigation hazardous. The gulf has
few good natural harbors.

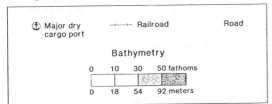

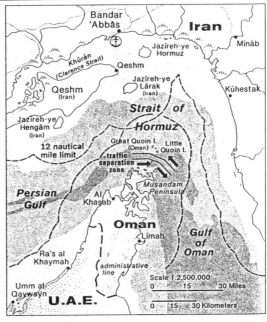

The Persian Gulf.

5 THE METEOROLOGICAL OCEAN

Scientists have studied the atmosphere for many decades, but its problems continue to defy us. The reasons for our limited progress are obvious. Weather cannot be easily reproduced and observed in the laboratory. It must, therefore, be studied in all of its violence wherever it has its way. Here, as in oceanography, new scientific tools have become available. With modern computers, rockets, and satellites, the time is ripe to harness a variety of disciplines for a concerted attack.

President John F. Kennedy

How do meteorologists study weather?

In the fifth century, Greek philosophers were tantalized by questions pertaining to nature. They believed that Earth, Atmosphere (air), Water, and Fire were the four basic forms of matter, which interacted to comprise all of nature. Recognizing the fundamental truth of this belief, the interdisciplinary science of meteorology now draws heavily on the basic concepts and techniques of other sciences, and especially oceanography, to understand how various characteristics of the Earth, Atmosphere, Water (of the oceans), and Fire (of the sun) interact to influence regional and global weather changes. The ability to predict such changes is the central goal of meteorology.

113

Modern weather prediction began in the first 35 years of the twentieth century when Vilhelm Bjerkes (1862–1952), Lewis F. Richardson (1881–1953), and John Von Neumann (1903–1957) each made major contributions to what is now termed *numerical forecasting.* Applying their knowledge of physics and mathematics to an understanding of some of the physical processes that take place in the atmosphere, they expressed these as mathematical equations and developed analytical methods for their solution. The resulting (numerical) solutions were used to predict weather conditions. These were based on changes reported in wind fields, pressure, and temperature. But their predictions were, at best, of limited accuracy and practical use, because of the relatively little information about the ocean that was available at the time, as well as the lack of computing machines.

This situation changed shortly after World War II. First, the electronic computer was developed, which alleviated much of the computational burden. Also, work in ocean science began to fill in some of the gaps of information about how the atmosphere and the ocean affect each other and the weather. And now marine meteorology furnishes many of the data and scientific advances regarding the various processes at work in the ocean.

Several large oceanographic study programs, coordinating satellite measurements and those taken on site, are now being carried out. The World Ocean Circulation Experiment and the Tropical Ocean and Global Atmosphere and Global Flux study are programs that recognize that changes in the atmosphere are tied to those in the ocean. Accordingly, their focus is on the exchange of heat, mass, and momentum between the ocean and the atmosphere.

Marine meteorologists use data sent to them by ships, weather buoys, aircraft, and satellites. These data help them

- Describe the general circulation of the ocean.
- Observe the oceanic transport of climatically and biologically important chemicals and materials, such as carbon.
- Determine seasonal oceanic variability on a global scale.

Launching a weather balloon. *(Courtesy Environmental Science Services Administration [ESSA])*

- Describe surface conditions and exchanges of physical properties with the atmosphere and detect any uncertainties.
- Obtain quantitative estimates of the exchange of chemical constituents between the upper-water ocean layer and the ocean interior, by identifying the properties of the surface layer.
- Determine oceanic heat transport and storage in relation to the earth's heat budget. (The earth's climate is controlled primarily by the amount of solar heat that the earth retains and by the transport of that heat from one region to another by the ocean and by the atmosphere.)
- Identify the important processes and balances in the general circulation.
- Construct numerical models for the diagnosis, simulation, and prediction of the ocean's general circulation.

In summary, atmospheric and ocean interactions are major factors in determining the weather. Meteorologists are now improving their predictions of long- and short-term weather conditions and the ways of modifying weather. This ability to predict weather conditions, both regional and global, has far-reaching applications. For example, storms started by the interaction of the ocean and the atmosphere can influence weather throughout the world. Thus, even activities in the middle of the continent— as well as those in, on, and around the ocean—can profit greatly by accurate forecasts, by enabling better preparation for weather extremes.

What is the hydrologic (or water) cycle?

The hydrologic cycle is the continuous transformation and movement of water by means of evaporation, precipitation, runoff, and return to the ocean. Water evaporates from the oceans and other bodies of water and from the leaves of growing plants.

It is then carried as a gas (or water vapor) to the atmosphere and leaves the atmosphere as precipitation, or rain. When the rain first falls, it is at its purest. But during its fall it picks up dust, chemical pollutants emitted from industrial operations and automobiles, salt carried inland from ocean spray, and carbon dioxide, which increases water's solvent action.

Moisture drawn up to the atmosphere also may return to the ocean directly as rain or snow, although most of it falls on land. Indeed, it is estimated that some 9000 cubic miles of water fall on land surfaces each year. On land the rain may reinforce the water table and augment the streams and rivers that transport dissolved minerals—along with sand, mud, silt, gravel, and rocks—back to the ocean. Some of the water from the atmosphere may be taken out of the cycle by being locked up as ice, and some evaporates back into the atmosphere and falls again as rain or snow.

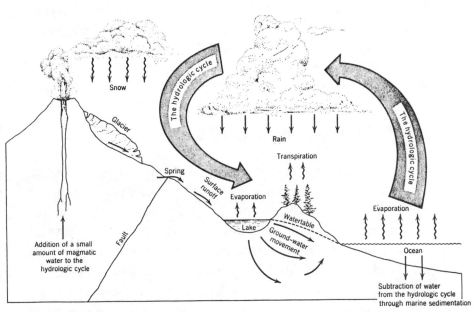

The hydrologic cycle.

What are the unique properties of water?

Because water covers about 70 percent of the earth and per-meates its atmosphere, it is not rare, although its properties are unique: Water is the only substance on earth that exists naturally as a liquid, solid, and gas. As a liquid, it has the ability to dissolve more materials and in greater quantities than any other liquid can. In its solid or frozen form, the density of water is less than that of its liquid form. This unusual property (and one shared only by the elements of bismuth, antimony, and gallium) was of pivotal importance to the development of life on earth. For if frozen water or ice had been denser than liquid water, then whenever freshwater bodies (or those containing fewer than 1000 parts of dissolved salts per million parts of water) froze, they would have frozen from bottom to top, as the newly formed ice at the cooled surface sank, and this would have eliminated the life-sustaining liquid water at the bottom. Water is, according to the fifteenth-century Italian artist Leonardo da Vinci, "the driver of nature." That is, without water in the atmosphere, there would be no weather.

What causes hurricanes?

Hurricanes are powerful storms with winds at least 75 miles per hour and often as much as 125 to 200 miles per hour. In the center or "eye" of the storm is a dead calm area where the barometric pressure is at its lowest. This eye is about 10 to 15 miles in diameter and is surrounded by a wall of clouds in which the winds are very high.

Hurricanes (the name is taken from *hurrican*, the Carib Indian word for evil spirit) originate in the tropical regions of the

A satellite view of a typhoon. *(Courtesy National Aeronautics and Space Administration [NASA])*

Atlantic, Pacific and Indian oceans, in open ocean areas where two air masses converge and the temperature of the ocean water is at least 79° F. Warm, moist air is drawn up from the ocean surface in a slow circular motion (caused by the earth's rotation) where it is cooled and water vapor condenses into the air. As the air spirals upward, through and out of a chimney of cooler air, it draws into it more of the warm air below. This self-perpetuating process intensifies the circulation, causing the hurricane to increase in size.

Hurricanes and typhoons are alike in origin, structure, and features, their only difference being the area of the world in which they occur. Hurricanes occur in the waters adjacent to North America (North Atlantic Ocean, Gulf of Mexico, Caribbean Sea, and southeastern North Pacific Ocean), and typhoons occur in the western North Pacific Ocean. Their prediction and tracking are now enhanced by photographs taken from satellites.

What are tsunamis, and what causes them?

A *tsunami* (Japanese for "harbor wave") is an ocean wave caused by sudden, large motion of a portion of the ocean floor or the shore, such as that caused by an earthquake, volcanic eruption, or landslide. A tsunami that overflows the land is popularly called a tidal wave, although it has no relation to the tide.

If a volcanic eruption occurs below the surface of the ocean, the escaping gases will cause water to be pushed upward in the shape of a dome or mound. The same effect is caused by the sudden rising of a portion of the ocean bottom. As this water settles back, it creates a wave that travels at high speed across the surface of the ocean.

In deep water the height of a tsunami is probably never greater than 2 or 3 feet. The distance between the waves is usually more than 100 miles, and in the Pacific, where most tsunamis occur, the speed of the wave is more than 400 knots (1 knot is a speed unit of 1 nautical mile—6112 feet—per hour). Although the waves produced are relatively small in the deep ocean, they can become extremely large and destructive as they approach shallow water and run up on the shore. Tsunamis 50 feet or higher over the shore have caused widespread damage in many areas.

Probably the most disastrous tsunami took place in 1883, when the volcano of Krakatau, between the islands of Java and Sumatra, blew up, sending out gigantic waves up to 115 feet high that swept away 1000 villages on nearby islands and killed 36,000 people. Almost equally destructive was the tsunami that roared into the Sanriku district of Japan, in 1896, destroying 13,000

Damage to a beachfront from a tsunami. *(Courtesy U.S. Navy)*

houses and killing 27,122 persons. Fifty years later, on April 1, 1946, a submarine earthquake near the Aleutian Islands caused a tsunami that spread over the entire Pacific. Scotch Cap Light on Unimak Island, 57 feet above sea level, was completely destroyed. Traveling at an average speed of 490 miles per hour, the waves reached the Hawaiian Islands in 4 hours and 34 minutes, where they arrived as waves 50 feet above the high-water level and flooded a strip of coast more than 1000 feet wide in some places. They left a death toll of 173 and property damage of $25 million. Less destructive waves reached the shores of North and Latin America and Australia, 6,700 miles from the epicenter.

After this disaster, a tsunami warning system was set up in the Pacific, even though destructive waves are relatively rare (averaging about one in 20 years in the Hawaiian Islands). Tsunamis have also been felt in Portugal, the Mediterranean, and other parts of the world such as the Japanese coast, which is the most frequently hit of all the Pacific coasts. On the average, a wave 25 feet high is recorded in Japan once every 15 years.

 ## What is El Niño?

Ocean currents and marine life are so interrelated that currents can sometimes be traced by their supply of plankton, the tiny floating plants and animals that are important food sources for fish and other ocean animals. In general, the oceanic circulation helps sustain marine life by stirring up the chemical nutrients in the water and carrying them, or the plankton formed from them, into regions that have an inadequate supply. However, this process can also be reversed. A notable example occurs from time to time off the west coast of Latin America. At unpredictable yearly intervals, an abnormally warm ocean current appears off the coast of Ecuador and Peru around Christmas time. This El Niño (Spanish for "child") current replaces the colder surface water, which is rich in chemical nutrients and plankton. The result is a radical change in the ecosystems. In 1982–1983, El Niño caused the wholesale destruction of fish and seabirds as well as major floods in Ecuador and Peru.

El Niños or, as scientists refer to them, ENSOs (El Niño–southern oscillations), are still difficult to forecast—when they will occur and how strong and destructive they will become. Although there are theories regarding how these phenomena start, it is still not known why some El Niños grow large in size and others do not. In 1924, Sir Gilbert Walker, of the British Meteorological Office in India, pointed out that atmospheric pressures over Australia are high when they are low off the coast of Latin America, and vice versa. This flip-flop of atmospheric pressure between the eastern and western Pacific, a reversal of the trade winds that usually blow across the tropical Pacific toward Asia, and other effects are climatic events that ocean meteorologists call the southern oscillation.

This oscillation now has been shown to be related to fluctuations in the ocean currents of the equatorial Pacific. When the trade winds are strong, equatorial waters flood into the western Pacific, and when the wind velocities slacken, warm surface waters flood back into the eastern Pacific. Here the rising of water from a lower level to a higher level or the upwelling of nutrient-rich water from the Peru current is depressed by horizontal submarine waves (Kelvin waves from the equator). Abnormally warm water accumulates along the coasts of Peru and Ecuador, causing an El Niño and raising the sea level of the area.

Since the 1982–1983 El Niño disaster that took many lives and caused billions of dollars in damage, a rudimentary monitoring system has now been established to alert scientists to atmospheric and oceanic changes in the Pacific Ocean that may herald major climate aberrations. Several buoys are strategically moored and equipped with sensors to take periodically the ocean's temperatures from the surface to 1600 feet and to gather wind and ocean current readings. This information is monitored by satellites and surface ships. Scientists also use instruments showing the structure of the thermocline—the sharp boundary between the ocean's warm surface layer and the cold deep layers.

When was the first weather satellite launched?

Satellites now provide meteorologists with much of the observational data needed for weather predictions. In 1960, a weather satellite, *Tiros,* the Television and Infrared Observation Satellite, gave meteorologists their first view of the earth, and its cloud cover, from space. Since that time, several weather satellites have been launched, providing valuable data regarding physical, biological, chemical, and geological processes of the earth that influence weather. In 1988, eleven civilian operational satellites from five different countries (United States, Soviet Union, Japan, India, and France) furnished such information. The remote imaging sensing of the earth by these satellites is tied into powerful computers that transmit the information in digital form, which when interpreted reveal the needed knowledge about the several forces that create our environment. From 1989 to 1992, the Navy Remote Ocean Sensing System Satellite (NROSS) and the European Resources Satellite (ERS-1) will also be in service to give meteorologists still more information about these forces.

A satellite view of clouds over the United States. *(Courtesy NOAA)*

THE ENGINEER'S OCEAN

> We should be concerned about the future be-
> cause we will have to spend the rest of our
> lives there.
>
> Charles F. Kettering

What is ocean engineering, and what do ocean engineers do?

Engineering is the application of mathematics, science, and technology to use economically the materials and forces of nature and thus to benefit society. Ocean engineering is that branch of engineering concerned with the design, construction, maintenance, and operation of structures, equipment, tools, devices, and systems to explore and develop the ocean's resources.

Ocean engineers are becoming increasingly capable of solving many problems regarding our judicious use of the ocean, such as the control of corrosion and fouling methods of mining the ocean floor for oil, gas, and minerals; techniques of recovering energy from the ocean; the control of beach erosion; new and improved oceanographic instrumentation; and techniques for reducing ocean pollution.

An oil platform off the coast of Louisiana. *(Courtesy Exxon, "An Exxon Photo")*

 What problems do ocean engineers face?

The ocean represents a real challenge to ocean engineers. They must select materials and design equipment that can be used successfully in and around saltwater. In addition, surface waters are almost everywhere in motion and can create considerable and unpredictable amounts of energy. When equipment is immersed in the ocean, it is subjected to water temperatures that range from about 68°F at 600 feet, to 41°F at 4000 feet, and the low thirties in the deepest regions. Over a temperature range of 30° to 68°F, the conductivity of the water—an important consideration in the corrosion of materials—almost doubles. With higher water temperatures (about 59°F), engineering materials are most vulnerable to ocean corrosion damage and fouling.

Ocean water is corrosive because it contains dissolved salts, which enable the water to conduct electricity. Metals immersed

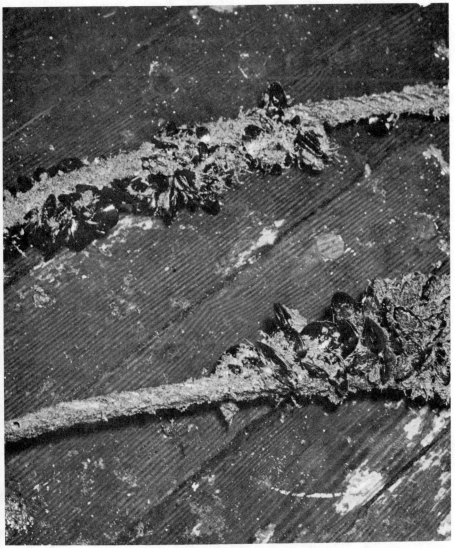

An example of corrosion and fouling (by barnacles).

in the ocean create an electric current in much the same way as in an automobile battery. This current conducts particles away from the metal, thus dissolving it. The use of stainless steel and protective coatings on the metals have helped alleviate some of this problem. Materials are also vulnerable to several insidious forms of corrosion, many of which, such as stress corrosion, are not yet fully understood. Even such materials as high-strength steels and titanium, which otherwise have desirable properties, sometimes exhibit low resistance to stress corrosion and fatigue.

What kinds of materials do ocean engineers favor?

All engineers seek to use materials with reliable, uniform, and reproducible properties for their designs. In the past, because of some of the ill-understood facets of the ocean's behavior and the behavior of materials placed in it, ocean engineers tended to be a conservative lot. They were either constrained to develop designs for needed ocean engineering work or were forced to employ what is known as the "brute force" design approach, an over-design method that was usually characterized by weight penalties to the equipment and structures and/or resulted in inefficient and costly operation.

Materials in underwater structures can fail for various reasons, including fatigue failure, buckling, stress corrosion, and ductile or brittle fracture. This fracture can be catastrophic. A cable snaps, a pipeline breaks in half, a submerged vessel bursts. The subject of fracture has been studied ever since entire ship hulls fractured during World War II, but nonetheless, the degree of success in developing materials with greater fracture resistance is still somewhat limited. There is also a need to understand how the ocean environment affects both stress corrosion cracking and corrosion fatigue in most materials and how fatigue is affected by weldments and other treatments.

In addition, anything placed in the ocean must be able to withstand pressures that increase by nearly 0.445 pounds of pressure per square inch for every foot of depth. This hydrostatic pressure represents a "squeezing" force or compressive loading on underwater structures, which is one reason for considering the use of brittle materials (such as ceramics and glassy materials), as they can withstand very high compressive loads. For example, glass fails not because of compression but because of tensile forces (or longitudinal stresses).

Thus, when designing underwater structures, it is necessary to guard against such tensile forces. They may occur with materials of strong compressive strength because of local bending near the structural stiffeners of vessels, or from an elastic deformation in cavities within the materials themselves. Tensile stresses may also follow upsets in the material caused by compression. Or hydrostatic pressure, combined with certain factors that induce motion in the ocean, may be translated into tension. Accordingly, various atmospheric forces above the ocean, manufactured and natural underwater phenomena, and turbulences must somehow be compensated.

Compounding this is the need for high strength-to-weight-ratio materials. Both operational and research submarine vehicles, for example, require strong hull materials yet still have the proper degree of buoyancy. That is, the hull materials must be both light and strong at the same time.

Steels, especially those called HY (high-yield) steels, have been used to satisfy submarine requirements. These steels can be welded; their main constraint is their weight. Titanium, with a yield strength of 100,000 pounds per square inch, is stronger than steel, yet weighs 40 percent less and has good anticorrosion characteristics.

Among the other materials used in ocean engineering designs

An instrument case made of chemically strengthened glass and a high-strength titanium ring. *(Courtesy Corning Glass Works)*

are quenched and tempered steels, maraging steels (alloys of iron, nickel, cobalt, molybdenum, and titanium with low carbon content), titanium-based alloys, and aluminum alloys (especially the 7000 series alloys, Al-Zn-Mg-Cu). Some of the other materials used are fiberglass-reinforced plastics, composite materials, concrete, glass, and other ceramics.

Composite structural materials are made from metals, ceramics, and polymers that are reinforced by fibers or metal or ceramic particles. For example, fibers (such as silicon carbide or silicon nitride) are added to form a MMC (metal matrix composite). PMCs are polymers (plastics) reinforced with graphite (carbon) fibers, themselves reinforced with an epoxy (resin). PMCs are up to four times as strong and stiff as steel and titanium (measured along the direction of fiber reinforcement) but are up to 50 percent lighter in weight. PMCs have been used for years in sonar domes on submarines and in radomes for surface ships. Although the physical and mechanical properties of composites are impressive, their greatest advantage is that they are "tailored" materials; that is, they are made up to have the properties required for a given application. Furthermore, a composite structure can be designed so that it has different properties in different directions or locations. By the judicious use of fiber or other reinforcement, strength or stiffness can be enhanced only in those locations where it is most needed, thereby enabling great efficiencies of design and cost.

How do engineers extract energy from the ocean?

The answer is that with a few exceptions, they do not. However, the ocean is loaded with energy in the form of heat, currents, tides, and waves. Although many ideas have been suggested for tapping these sources of power, few have ever been put into practice. The reasons are mainly the high cost of building a workable system and the consequence that the power (such as tidal power) cannot compete economically with that produced by nuclear fission and other methods.

Nevertheless, the energy of the oceans is impressive. For example, it is estimated that 4-foot waves striking a coast 10 seconds apart expend more than 35,000 horsepower per mile of coast. Some attempts were made in Algeria to harness this wave energy, by funneling the waves into a reservoir through a V-shaped structure made of concrete. The water flowing out of the reservoir operates a turbine that generates power. Wave power also has been used in Japan to power lighthouses. Another concept uses temperature differences in ocean waters. In 1814, Alexander von Humboldt observed that water in the ocean is cold (40°F) at various deep depths in the tropics and warm (77°F) at the surface. He explained this as the result of the sinking and outflow of surface water in the polar regions. In 1881, D'Arsonval suggested that people would someday be able to mine this surface heat to help power their civilization. In the 1930s, such temperature differences in the ocean were exploited to try to run a water vapor turbine. But these attempts were unsuccessful, and the idea was abandoned until the mid-1970s. At that time, several U.S. engineers envisioned a design in which massive volumes of the warm surface water in various parts of the ocean could be used to vaporize a volatile fluid like ammonia or propane. This action could then be used to drive power-plant turbines. The vapors would be condensed back into fluid form by the cold waters from lower depths and then recycled through the turbines. This idea of generating electricity continuously to a mainland location by means of cables still has some technical problems (such as fouling and environmental impact) to be solved. However, the concept has been tried in Hawaii and may well become a way of constructing power plants capable of generating from the ocean 500 million watts or more of electricity.

Another, less publicized ocean energy scheme is a mash

method of converting seaweed (such as kelp) into fuels—oil, gasoline, and natural gas. Kelp can also be used to produce various chemicals, drugs, and foods.

In regard to using the tides for power, there are only a few places in the world where the variations in high and low tides are large enough to be harnessed. In two areas the tidal range is great enough to pursue this objective economically: Passamaquoday Bay, Maine, and St. Malo, France. But even if these and the other candidate areas of the world were utilized, they could supply only about one-tenth of 1 percent of the world's power requirements by the year 2000.

Among the several other suggestions and ideas for harnessing some of this energy is one that would use the Florida current. The stream energy in this current, located off the east coast of Florida, would be captured via some mechanism to generate electricity in a cost-effective way. This power could then be used in the electrolysis of distilled water to produce hydrogen, a synthetic and clean fuel, and oxygen. The hydrogen produced could also be used to synthesize hydrocarbon fuels from various sources of carbon, including carbon dioxide in the atmosphere. Whatever the eventual outcome of such ideas and operations, among the most salient problems facing the world today are the shortage of energy, the depletion of fossil fuel sources, and the increasing pollution, including acid rain and the warming of the earth by the so-called greenhouse effect. The oceans may hold the answers to these problems.

What is marine fouling?

Some ocean plants and animals—barnacles, seaweeds, worms, algae (blue-green), and other organisms—have the nasty habit of attaching themselves to the bottoms of ships, fixed offshore platforms, and underwater equipments, and structures. This "fouling" interferes in the operation and efficiency of, for example, underwater equipment such as sonar when the attached marine life interferes with the normal path of sound waves. These creatures also increase fixed or moored ocean structures' lateral resistances to currents and waves. Such organisms also can damage the protective coatings used on materials for corrosion protection.

Why are barnacles a problem?

The underwater surfaces of ships are especially susceptible to fouling when they are in port, the principal offenders being the ubiquitous acorn barnacles. After hatching from eggs within the shell of the adult, the barnacle larvae must swim to some surface such as a rock or a ship bottom. Here, they multiply and, with other attached organisms, make rough an otherwise smooth surface. This causes a drag or an increased skin frictional resistance to the movement of the ship when it is moving, which requires an increase in fuel or energy consumption.

Sailors have long battled the barnacle problem. First they put tar and copper strips on their ships' bottoms to discourage barnacles and to make rowing easier and sailing faster. For the past two decades, ships have used a number of antifoulant paints such as copper-based paints and tributyltin (TBT). These have been quite effective, but they contain toxic substances that leach into the water and kill various valuable marine organisms, including oysters, lobsters, and fish.

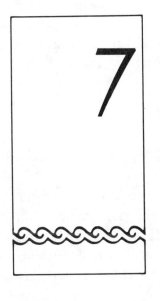

THE GLOBAL OCEAN—PAST, PRESENT, AND FUTURE

The sea merely lies in wait for the innocent,
but it stalks the careless and the ignorant.
Admiral George W. Anderson, Jr.,
U.S. Navy (retired)

 What is meant by the term "global ocean"?

The world ocean is the largest single geographical feature of our planet. Bounded only by land and air, it joins rather than separates people. The study of its complex biology, geology, meteorology, and physical and chemical characteristics is a large and varied task for all who wish to engage themselves in it. The ocean is also a place for recreational activities—swimming, surfing, sailing, and fishing. And for poets and artists it holds many attractions—the rise and fall of the tides, the endless progression of the waves, and the color of the waters. Inspired also by the dynamic ocean are historians who seek to understand the past, and adventurers who seek to recover the ocean's lost treasures.

How all these people interact with this global ocean depends, quite simply, on their attitudes, objectives, and technical abilities.

Do sea monsters exist?

It is doubtful that there are sea monsters, at least not the kind that people usually imagine. However, the giant squid *Architeuthis principes*, has a body that can be 15 feet wide, eight arms, and two much longer, thinner tentacles. Such a squid can weigh over a ton and, including tentacles, extend over 65 feet. Sightings of these creatures have given rise to some of the sea-serpent legends. But even though we know that such giant squid definitely exist, none has ever been captured.

What is Atlantis?

The story of Atlantis is one of the most interesting and persistent of all legends. At last count there are said to be 5000 scholarly publications about the lost Atlantian civilization. Most of these base their theories about the location of this civilization on certain possible geologic, biological, oceanographic and anthropological evidence.

The Greek philosopher Plato (427?–347? B.C.) first described Atlantis as a place inhabited by a people far ahead of their time. They built temples, ships, and canals and had an advanced agriculture and commerce. By 9600 B.C., as the story goes, they had conquered all the known world except Greece, which was saved when Atlantis was engulfed by the sea and disappeared without a trace. A myth? Perhaps not: Remember that for thousands of years the cities of Troy, Pompeii, and Herculaneum were considered to be mythical places.

Is there living evidence of Atlantis?

Although the biological evidence for an Atlantis in the middle of the North Atlantic is inconclusive, the flight pattern of certain migratory ocean birds and the odd behavior of the eels there are interesting. For instance, some migratory birds spend the summer in Europe and winter in Latin America. When flying from Europe they circle an area in the middle of the Atlantic several times, as though in search of land and, after failing to find it, go on to Brazil. Does this indicate some atavistic memory of a land region that was once there? Also, the eels, freshwater fish of eastern North American and European rivers, migrate to the ocean when spawning time draws near. They swim to the Sargasso Sea where they mate and die. Their offspring, the young eels, begin the return voyage: Those of American parentage go the rivers of North America, and those of European parentage go to the rivers of Europe, as far as 5000 to 7000 miles away! Are they equipped with some built-in mechanism of recall that tells them the Sargasso Sea had been closed off in the east by some nearby land in whose rivers eels once lived? The disappearance of such a landmass probably caused them to swim on, helped by the Gulf Stream, until they found the next-nearest land—Europe. The disproportionate distance between the gathering place of these separate species and their respective habitats is otherwise quite difficult to explain.

Who invented the first submarine?

The first successful submarine was built in the seventeenth century by a Dutch inventor, Cornelius Van Drebbel. Drebbel's craft, equipped with 12 oars, operated up and down under the Thames River for approximately 10 years. An American, Davis

Bushnell, built the first war submarine, the *Turtle*, during the American Revolution. Larger than most modern-day research submersibles, the *Turtle* had water-ballast tanks and pumps and two hand-operated screw propellers. In the beginning of the nineteenth century, another American, Robert Fulton, built the *Nautilus*, a submarine with a copper hull 21 feet long and 7 feet in diameter, diving planes, a hemispherical conning tower with glass lookouts, and a hand-operated propeller for propulsion.

Is there much interest today in the recovery of sunken ships and treasures?

The answer is yes. For many people, the attraction is personal wealth—gold and silver. For others, it is marine archaeology—or the systematic study of antiquities (ships, cities, relics, artifacts, and the like) found in the world's ocean—in order to reconstruct the past. And for some legislators and officials in the federal and state governments, it is the ownership or the control of the sunken property in the public interest.

Consider the Treasure Salvors, Inc. case. Mel Fisher and his company, Treasure Salvors, after searching the seventeenth-century wrecks of the *Atocha* and *Santa Margarita*, submerged some seven miles off Florida, recovered in the 1970s several million dollars worth of artifacts and treasure. However, the state of Florida claimed ownership of the wreck. Treasure Salvors asserted that in the case of an abandoned vessel, the finder assumes possession according to long-standing principles of maritime law. The state lost when federal courts upheld Treasure Salvors' claims.

Although the state of Florida is still not satisfied with this outcome, many objective observers believe that it is consistent with the United States' free enterprise system. Furthermore, they acknowledge that on balance, Fisher's salvaging operation was carried out intelligently and responsibly. In this regard, the work of two individuals associated with the operation merit special recognition: The first, Bill Muir, a qualified diver and structural engineering designer, studied and researched the recovered remains of the *Atocha* and *Santa Margarita* and then made detailed drawings of them. This in itself is a major accomplishment, as we have relatively little information about the construction of early seventeenth-century ships. It seems that most shipbuilders of that day carried the plans in their head. The other person worthy of recognition here is Duncan Matthewson, III. Matthewson, a competent and dedicated marine archaeologist, in his association with the Fisher operation carried out many tasks to minimize damage to the excavation sites. His work has been widely recognized.

Still some people say that this particular salvaging operation, though commendable, represents only one case. On the darker side of treasure recovery operations are several examples of vandalism, neglect, and the wanton destruction of the sites—all of which contain material valuable to the public.

A 1987 report by the U.S. Government's Office of Technology Assessment, "Technologies for Underwater Archaeology and Maritime Preservation," states:

> The public is often unaware of the crucial differences between treasure hunting, which focuses on historic objectives of high intrinsic cultural or economic value, and archeology, which focuses on the scientific understanding of the entire archaeological site within the context of its surroundings. In their attempts to recover artifacts quickly, treasure hunters both deliberately and inadvertently destroy much of the contextual information essential for advancing scientific knowledge. Improved education of the general public, and those whose activities might adversely affect significant sites, could result in a higher degree of protection.

The retrieval and study of sunken objects in the ocean is of special importance to marine archaeologists and historians, as

well as other specialists—engineers, biologists, chemists, phys-
icists, and geologists. For instance, their investigations can be
applied and combined in order to gain a better understanding of
how materials used to build ships and other things have changed
after being immersed in the ocean and subjected to its miscellaneous forces and resources. Although there is now no co-
herent national policy for underwater archaeology and treasure
salvaging, 27 states have passed statutes to broaden their jurisdiction and exert regulatory control over significant wrecks within
their territorial waters.

What are some of the most noteworthy underwater salvaging events?

Until shortly after World War II, even the shallow coastal
waters were inaccessible to those interested in recovering submerged wrecks and the cargos they contained; it has only been in
the last few years that we have had the tools to find and salvage
portions of these wrecks. A notable exception to this was the
work of Hans Albrect van Treibelen of Sweden and Andreas
Peckell of Germany. In 1664, they used a primitive diving bell in
110 feet of water to recover 50 bronze cannons from a 200-foot-
long Swedish warship, the *Wasa,* that had sunk some 36 years
before in Stockholm harbor. The recovery operation was a technical accomplishment unmatched until the latter part of the
twentieth century.

In 1901 and again in 1907, the Greek government hired
sponge divers to recover statues dating from the first century B.C.
from Roman shipwrecks off Tunis in the Bay of Mahdia. Several
statues and other artifacts from these ancient cargo ships were
successfully recovered.

After World War II, skin divers using the newly perfected Self-
Contained Underwater Breathing Apparatus (scuba) began

to bring up various objects of artistic value from ancient ships, most of which had sunk in the shallower waters of the Mediterranean.

Then, in 1958, Sweden's Neptune Salvaging Company decided to excavate the aforementioned ship, the *Wasa*. After three years of underwater work, the old warship of 1300 tons displacement (the weight of the water displaced by the ship) was brought to the surface on April 24, 1961. Per Lundstrom, the chief archaeologist of the *Wasa* excavation, and marine archaeologists throughout the world were thrilled by the many objects found aboard and by the ship. Many of the objects were remarkably well preserved, revealing an interesting cross section of life in 1628. Several hundred tons of polyethylene glycol, a preservative, were used on the ship's timbers to prevent them from drying out and cracking. The renovated and restored ship together with the many objects it carried is now on exhibition in a Stockholm museum.

Inspired by these archaeological discoveries, in the 1960s, George Bass, an archaeologist at the University of Pennsylvania, headed an expedition to recover cargo items from a ship that had sunk in 1200 B.C. off the coast of Turkey in the Cape Gelidonya area. The 18-man expedition team was composed of underwater archaeologists, photographers, draftsmen, and divers. They were successful not only in their work at Cape Gelidonya but also in excavating the wreck of another ship that had sunk in 100 feet of water in about A.D. 620 at Yassi Ada near Bodrum, Turkey.

But despite the success of a few people, hundreds more have spent large sums of money only to fail even to locate a sunken wreck, let alone to salvage any of its treasures.

The aforementioned Mel Fisher also spent millions of dollars over some 18 years of intensive underwater searching and recovery efforts. Such efforts were highlighted not only by his discovery and recovery of the contents of two seventeenth-century ships but also by litigation with the state of Florida and the federal government over the ownership of such property.

In the past decade, the discoveries, recoveries, and explorations of several sunken ships have largely been made possible by the use of many new technologies that were developed for other purposes. For instance, a sophisticated, remotely operated vehicle (ROV) mapped and explored the USS *Monitor*, a Civil War ironclad warship, which lies on the ocean bottom some 16 miles off Cape Hatteras. This ROV also recovered parts of the space shuttle *Challenger* from the ocean in 1986. The location and dramatic underwater filming in 1987 of the British luxury liner *Titanic* some two and a half miles below the surface was made possible by a variety of positional and recording devices and deep-water submersibles.

How are small manned submersibles and remotely controlled vehicles used in ocean research and engineering?

Small manned submersibles and remotely controlled vehicles (ROVs) first came into prominence in the 1960s. First, the bathyscaphe *Trieste* was used on January 23, 1960, to transport Jacques Piccard and Donald Walsh to a depth of over 35,000 feet at the bottom of the Challenger Deep (Marianas Trench), which is the deepest point in the ocean.

In 1963, the *Thresher* was the U.S. Navy's newest, fastest, deepest-diving, best-equipped nuclear submarine. But, during its trial cruise in April 1963 while approximately 8400 feet deep, the *Thresher* mysteriously (density differences between adjacent masses of water and extremely powerful subsurface waves probably contributed to the loss) sank to the ocean floor and was lost forever. The sub's disappearance challenged the United States' capability for deep-ocean rescue and salvage. It was only through the combined efforts of nearly every oceanographic facility and every major navy scientific facility, plus the *Trieste* and many

The **Trieste.** *(Courtesy U.S. Navy)*

surface ships that the wreckage of the *Thresher* was located and photographed. The search for the *Thresher* produced considerable oceanographic knowledge and led to techniques and methods for ocean engineering work, including data on submersible design.

Such knowledge and expertise proved invaluable in February, March, and April 1966, during the deep-sea search for a lost hydrogen bomb. For 228 hours between mid-February and early April 1966, the deep-water submersible *Alvin* searched the steep, rugged floor of the Mediterranean Sea off the coast of Palomares, Spain, for an H-bomb ejected by a disabled U.S. bomber. During this period, the *Alvin's* three pilots, working two at a time, put the craft through a series of unprecedented maneuvers while completing 34 dives to depths as great as 3000 feet. The average length of each dive was 7 hours, and the longest dive lasted 11 hours.

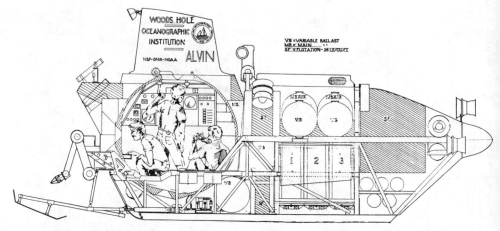

The **Alvin.** *(Courtesy WHOI)*

Despite such operating experience, the use of small manned submersibles and remotely controlled vehicles in ocean projects as practical, economic workstations has been accepted only since 1976. Between 1977 and 1987 they proved to be invaluable to a variety of underwater commercial operations. Technological improvements made it possible for small submersibles, carrying two or three people, to reach depths of 20,000 feet or more and to remain there for as long as two or three days if necessary. In the offshore oil and gas industries such submersibles have been used to construct, maintain, monitor, and repair equipment, and now they are beginning to be used more and more in ocean science research, including marine archeology.

Indeed, the submersibles' utility in marine archeology was demonstrated dramatically in 1986 when the wreck of the RMS *Titanic* (sunk in 1912 in waters 350 miles southwest of New Foundland) was discovered by the *Argo*, a tethered ROV equipped with sonar scanners, high-powered lights, and television cameras capable of viewing an acre of the ocean floor at a time. Later, the *Titanic*'s interior was explored in 13,000 feet of water by the small remotely operated craft, *Jason R.*, which was deployed from the *Alvin*.

Are surface ships still used for ocean research and engineering?

Surface ships have traditionally been used for conducting oceanographic research and ocean engineering work. The addition of new methods and improved instrumentation for such research has not replaced the need for ships but has identified new and productive ways to use them. Among their tasks are collecting physical and chemical samples of the ocean, the ocean floor, and the plant and animal life; deploying instruments in the ocean; and collecting data over a large ocean area. Research ships are also used to launch and support other vehicles, submersibles, data buoys, remotely operated stations, and diving systems.

Before the 1960s the surface ships used for oceanographic research were vessels converted for this purpose, especially in the years following World War II when many surplus military ships were available. Such conversions were not entirely satisfactory, however. Recognizing this, the U.S. government in the late 1950s began to design a ship especially for research. During the 1960s, the national oceanographic fleet used many of these specially built ships and also introduced other types of ocean research platforms and specialized shoreside support facilities for these platforms. Manned submersibles, fixed platforms, specialized buoys, bottom crawlers, unmanned submersibles, satelllites and aircraft, and special vessels all added to the oceanographer's capabilities.

This same period also saw the development of a commercial oceanographic fleet. Before this time a few research ships were operated by the federal government, a few universities, and research stations. The new commercial vessels are engaged in offshore oil and gas research as well as fisheries and ocean mining research. In recent years, commercial research has been done in deep-sea mining in water depths as great as three miles.

Research platform operation, development, and management in the 1980s can best be summarized as nearly static. Since 1970, 10 new vessels have entered the university research fleet, but the total fleet size has shrunk from 35 to 25 vessels during this period. In this context, "university research fleet" means mainly government-funded (bur not necessarily government-owned) vessels.

How are satellites being used in oceanographic work today?

Satellites are being used to observe and measure from space many characteristics of the global ocean. Spurred by the launch in 1957 of the world's first artificial satellite, the Soviet Union's *Sputnik I*, the use of a growing range of satellites, sensors, and computers is adding to our knowledge of the ocean.

Since 1960, the planning, development, and operation of several meteorological and oceanographic mission-oriented satellites have been under the aegis of the United States' National Oceanic and Atmospheric Administration (NOAA) and the National Aeronautics and Space Administration (NASA).

Remote sensing of the ocean is made possible by equipping the satellites with optical or radar instruments. These instrument systems can provide detailed information from 500 to 600 miles above the earth on wave and wind conditions; water color, temperature, texture, and topography; coastal storms; and ice conditions. This information is then transmitted to the ground when the satellite is in range of a receiving station, and there now is a worldwide network of receiving stations. Such information is valuable not only to physical and meteorological oceanographers, in regard to their interests in winds, wave heights, ocean currents, and so on; it also is useful to ocean engineers planning offshore installations and operations. Marine biologists, too, profit from the satellites' color photographs, as the colors can be related to biological activity. For example, a deep-blue color indicates a sterile, clear open ocean, whereas the presence of increasing amounts of chlorophyll-bearing plants (phytoplankton) shows up as green and red. Such plants are at the base of the ocean food chains, and all animals in the ocean depend on their presence and growth. The fishing industry also uses information on the biological activity in various portions of the oceans.

Several new satellites for studying the ocean are planned. One of these, the ERS-1 (Earth Resources Satellite), which the European Space Agency intends to launch in 1990, will be capable of working in all kinds of weather and in both day and night. Other satellites planned for the 1990s are being designed to observe conditions and resources on the planet, which will be helpful for a number of applications, including oil exploration and the mapping and management of land and water resources.

How are computers used in ocean science and engineering?

Computers have been used in ocean research since they were first made available after World War II. In those days, vacuum tube–based computers were used in several tasks, such as predicting tides and storms. In the 1950s, semiconducting transistors revolutionized electronics. Transistors not only were much smaller and more reliable than the vacuum tubes they replaced, but they also consumed very little power. Subsequent innovations in transistors and the increasing ability to install complex logical functions on a single microprocessor chip led to solid-state technology, which has surged forward during the past ten years, revolutionizing the computer industry. Today, a new generation of high-speed, large-capability computers are available. These can be used to enlarge our understanding of the physical ocean and to apply it to such problems as climate, fishery management, long-range weather prediction, and the management and utilization of ocean resources.

﹈ What is the U.S. National Ocean Service?

The U.S. National Ocean Service, a unit of the National Oceanic and Atmospheric Administration (NOAA), is the U.S. government's oldest scientific and technical agency, having been established in 1807 to survey and chart the Atlantic coastal waters. The National Ocean Service has been best known for making nautical charts and predicting the times and heights of the high and low tides.

Among the many programs administered by the National Ocean Service are the National Estuarine Sanctuary Program, which provides funding to states and U.S. territories to acquire and manage estuaries for research and education. There currently are 15 national estuarine sanctuaries, including Narragansett Bay in Rhode Island, Appalachicola Bay and River in Florida, Waimanu in Hawaii, and Padilla Bay in Washington.

The National Marine Sanctuary Program designates and manages offshore marine areas to preserve or restore their natural resources. A management plan for each site, including research and educational programs, ensures that these special marine areas are used for the long-term benefit of the public. There currently are six national marine sanctuaries—the Channel Islands off the coast of southern California, Gray's Reef off the coast of Georgia, Key Largo south of Florida, the Point Reyes–Farallon Islands off the coast of northern California, Looe Key off Florida's Big Pine Key, and the site of the sunken wreck of the famous Civil War iron-clad USS *Monitor* off the coast of North Carolina.

The Monitor. *(Courtesy U.S. Navy)*

What are the trends in ocean recreation?

The beaches and coastal waters of the ocean offer a matchless opportunity for recreation. But the greater number of people and more available leisure time for most Americans has increased the demands on the capacities of many of these recreational areas. Moreover, in some areas the beaches are giving way (or already have) to industrial and residential development. In addition, tides, currents, and waves have shortened the beaches. Others have been contaminated by pollution. To maximize the good and minimize the bad, many people believe that the government should

- prohibit the building of homes, hotels, and condominiums on land that is definitely unsuitable for such uses but more suitable as a recreational zone.

- aggressively pursue means of preventing the pollution and erosion of the coastal waters.
- encourage the development of ocean recreational parks and reserves.
- provide various services to the areas, such as the coast guard, navigational aids, weather warning signals, and the search and rescue of small sailing and power vessels.

What does the future hold for ocean science and engineering?

Although scientific and engineering interest in the ocean has waxed and waned over most of the past 150 years, the progress made in the past three decades has been remarkable. A relatively small number of dedicated people have studied and worked with the ocean long enough to believe in its great potential. Because of their efforts, scientists and engineers now work together in several ocean programs. Research teams from government, industry, and academia frequently share information gathered from a variety of technologies, ranging from sample bottles to satellites. As a result, many puzzles that appeared unsolvable in the 1950s are now yielding to powerful investigative tools and techniques. Nonetheless, many of these discoveries have raised more questions than they have answered. Some of these questions may be answered in the future by means of new technologies that are being developed for other fields but that can be adapted to ocean investigations and ocean resource-utilization work. Already, computers, space satellites, new and improved instrumentation and equipment, remote operated vehicles, submersibles, improved research ships, aircraft, ocean data systems, buoys, and moored systems all have contributed to our present knowledge about the ocean.

Although it certainly is risky to try to predict the future, it is certain that the future of ocean science and engineering depends on the attitudes, objectives, and technical abilities of people. These include not only the oceanographers and ocean engineers but also people with an understanding and appreciation of the ocean and its potential, people with good ideas on how best to realize such potential, and new people from groups and institutions that have not traditionally been a part of ocean science and engineering. With their help, our growing knowledge of the ocean will help create new, and improved technological applications that can bring higher levels of individual and national security, productivity, satisfaction and well being.

 TABLES

TABLE 1
Distances, Areas, Volumes, and Weights

1 inch = 2.54 centimeters

1 square inch = 6.45 square centimeters

1 cubic inch = 16.39 cubic centimeters

1 centimeter = 0.39 inches

1 square centimeter = 0.15 square inches

1 cubic centimeter = 0.06 cubic inches

1 foot = 0.30 meters

1 square foot = 0.09 square meters

1 cubic foot = 0.03 cubic meters

1 meter = 3.28 feet

1 square meter = 10.76 square feet

1 cubic meter = 35.31 cubic feet

1 yard = .91 meters

1 square yard = 0.84 square meters

1 cubic yard = 0.76 cubic meters

1 meter = 1.09 yards

1 square meter = 1.20 square yards

1 cubic meter = 1.31 cubic yards

1 are = 100 square meters = 119.6 square yards

1 statute mile = 0.86 nautical miles

1 square statute mile = 0.74 square nautical miles

1 statute mile = 1.61 kilometers

1 square statute mile = 2.59 square kilometers

1 nautical mile = 1.16 statute miles

1 square nautical mile = 1.35 square statute miles

1 nautical mile = 1.85 kilometers

1 square nautical mile = 3.43 square kilometers

1 kilometer = 0.62 statute miles

1 square kilometer = 0.39 square statute miles

1 kilometer = 0.54 nautical miles

1 square kilometer = 0.29 square nautical miles

1 short ton = 2000 pounds = 0.91 metric tons

1 long ton = 2240 pounds = 1.02 metric tons

1 metric ton = 1.10 short tons = 0.98 long tons

TABLE 2
Some Facts about the Earth and the Ocean

EARTH

Circumference (at the Equator) ....24,901 mi.
Circumference (at the Meridian) ....24,860 mi.
Polar Diameter ....7,900 mi.
Equatorial Diameter ....7,926 mi.
Area of Surface ....196,939,000 mi.
Mass .... 6,588,000,000,000,000,000,000 tons
Volume ....259,878,000,000 cu. mi.
Mean Distance to Moon ....238,854 mi.
Mean Distance to Sun............................92,900,000 mi.
Surface Area Covered by Land ....55,000,000 mi.
Mean Orbital Velocity (Distance per Second) ....18.51 mi.

OCEAN

Surface Area Covered by Oceans ....(approx.) 142,000,000 sq. mi.
Volume ....(approx.) 326,000,000 cu. mi.
Greatest Depth.....................................35,000 + ft.
Largest Ocean (Pacific) ....63,800,000 sq. mi.
Total Weight of Ocean Water..... (Approx.) 1.45×10^{18} tons or 0.022
Percent of the Earth's Total Weight

TABLE 3
Some Properties of Ocean Water

PROPERTY	DESCRIPTION
Salinity	The amount of the dissolved solid material in the water. Usually expressed in partial salinity units (psu) or in parts per thousand (ppt), by weight, under standard conditions. Ocean salinity generally varies from about 33 to 37 ppt., with the average being about 35 ppt..
Chlorinity	The approximate amount of chlorine in the water. It is about 55 percent of the salinity, with an average of around 19 ppt.
Temperature	Varies widely in the ocean, both horizontally and vertically. At the surface the temperature of the water varies from 96°F (35.6°C) in the Persian Gulf in the summer to 28.5°F (−2°C) in the White Sea. The vertical distribution nearly everywhere shows a decrease of temperature with depth, although a freak geothermal temperature of 132.8°F (56°C) was recorded in February 1965 near the bottom of the 7200-ft. Discovery Deep in the Red Sea. The normal sea temperature in this area is 71.6° (22°C).
Pressure	Usually expressed in atmosphere or cgs (centimeter–gram–second) units. The principal cgs pressure unit is dyne per cm², and 1 million dyne per cm² = 1 bar (0.1 bar = 1 decibar). The decibar is the hydrostatic pressure exerted on 1 square centimeter of surface by 1 meter of ocean water. Hydrostatic pressure increases by 1 decibar with every meter of depth, or about 1 psi of pressure is added for each 2.25 feet of depth.
Viscosity	Resistance to flow. Ocean water is slightly more viscous than freshwater is. Its viscosity increases with greater salinity, but the effect is not nearly as marked as that occurring with decreasing temperature.
Compressibility	For ocean water, only 0.000046 per bar under standard conditions, varying slightly with changes of temperature or salinity. The effect of compression is to force the molecules of a substance closer together, thus causing it to become more dense. Even if the compressibility is low, its total effect will be considerable because of the amount of water involved. That is, if the compressibility of ocean water were zero, sea level would be about 90 feet higher than it is now.

PROPERTY	DESCRIPTION
Density	Mass per unit volume. Oceanographers use the cgs system, in which density is expressed as grams per cubic centimeter. The ratio of the density of a particular substance to that of a standard substance under stated conditions is called *specific gravity*. By definition, the density of distilled water at 4°C (39° .2F) is 1 gram per milliliter (approximately 1 gram per cubic centimeter). Therefore, if this is used as the standard, as it is in oceanographic work, density and specific gravity will be virtually identical numerically.

The density of ocean water depends on its salinity, temperature, and pressure. At a constant temperature and pressure, density varies with salinity or, because of the relationship between this and chlorinity, with the chlorinity. The density at a particular pressure is important to its relation to ocean currents.

The greatest changes in the density of ocean water occur at the surface, where the water is subject to influences not present farther down. Here density is decreased by precipitation, runoff from land, melting ice, or heating. When the surface water becomes less dense, it tends to float on top of the more dense water below. The density of surface water is increased by evaporation, formation of ice, and cooling. If the surface water becomes more dense than that below, it will sink to a layer of water with the same density. Here it tends to spread out to form a layer, or to increase the thickness of the layer below it.

The less dense water rises to make room for it, and the surface water moves to replace that which has descended. Thus, a convective circulation is established, which continues until the density becomes uniform from the surface to the depth at which a greater density occurs. If the surface water becomes sufficiently dense, it will sink all the way to the bottom. If this occurs in an area where horizontal flow is unobstructed, the water that has descended will spread to other regions, creating a dense bottom layer. Because the greatest increase in density occurs in polar regions, where the air is cold and great quantities of ice form, the cold, dense polar water sinks to the bottom and then spreads to lower latitudes. This process continues until the entire ocean floor is covered with this dense polar water.

TABLE 4

Elements Present in Solution in Oceanic Seawater of Chlorinity = 19.00 ‰, (given by weight in parts per million, exclusive of dissolved gases)

ELEMENT	PARTS PER MILLION	ELEMENT	PARTS PER MILLION	ELEMENT	PARTS PER MILLION
Chlorine	18,980	Lithium	0.1	Cerium	0.0004
Sodium	10,561	Phosphorus	0.001–0.10	Silver	0.0003
Magnesium	1,272	Barium	0.05	Vanadium	0.0003
Sulphur	884	Iodine	0.05	Lanthanum	0.0003
Calcium	400	Arsenic	0.01–0.02	Yttrium	0.0003
Potassium	380	Iron	0.002–0.02	Nickel	0.0001
Bromine	65	Manganese	0.001–0.01	Scandium	0.00004
Carbon	28	Copper	0.001–0.01	Mercury	0.00003
Strontium	13	Zinc	0.005	Gold	0.000006
Boron	4.6	Lead	0.004	Radium	$0.2–3 \times 10^{-10}$
Silicon	0.02–4.0	Selenium	0.004	Cadmium	trace
Fluorine	1.4	Cesium	0.002	Cobalt	trace
Nitrogen	0.006–0.7	Uranium	0.0015	Tin	trace
Aluminium	0.5	Molybdenum	0.0005		
Rubidium	0.2	Thorium	0.0005		

TABLE 5
Animal Forms in the Ocean

DIVISION	SYSTEM OR PROVINCE	ZONE	ECOLOGICAL GROUPS	PLANT AND ANIMAL FORMS
Benthic	Littoral	Littoral Sublittoral	Benthos (seafloor animals)	1. Sessile (Sponges, mussels, oysters, (immobile) crinoids, corals, hydroids, bryozoans, barnacles) Tube worms Seaweeds and sea grasses Diatoms 2. Creeping forms (crabs, lobsters, copepods, amphipods) Crustaceans Protozoans Snails Bivalves 3. Burrowing forms (clams, worms) Crustraceans Echinoderms
	Deep-sea	Bathyal Abyssal Hadal		
Pelagic	Neritic Oceanic	Epipelagic Mesopelagic	Nekton (swimming animals) Plankton (floating animals or floating plants)	Floating and Drifting Life 1. Zooplankton (feebly swimming or floating animals) 2. Phytoplankton (microscopic floating plants)

Source: U.S. Navy publication

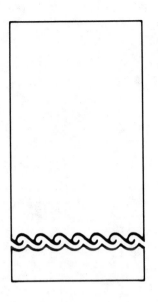

GLOSSARY

The following brief definitions of some ocean science and engineering terms are given to supplement terms and information contained in this book. The definition are not intended to be comprehensive but, rather, to serve as a convenient reference.

Abyssal plain
A flat or gently sloping region of the deep (generally below 12,000 feet) ocean floor.

Active margin
The leading edge of a continental plate characterized by coastal volcanic mountain ranges, frequent earthquake activity, and relatively narrow continental shelves.

Agulhas current
An Indian Ocean current along the southeast coast of Africa.

Algae
A group of lower photosynthetic plants varying greatly in color and habitat. They exist on land or in water and range in size from very tiny one-celled species to large forms such as kelp.

165

Alluvial

Referring to alluvium (sand, silt, or similar disintegrated material deposited by running water that can no longer transport it.

Antarctic Ocean

Those portions (5.731 million square miles) of the Atlantic, Pacific, and Indian oceans that border Antarctica on the south and the subtropical convergence on the north.

Atlantic Ocean

The 31.53 million square miles of ocean area, including the North Polar Sea, bordered by the continents of the Americas, Europe, and Africa. The northern boundary between the Atlantic and Pacific oceans is the Bering Strait. The shortest line from Cape Horn to the South Shetland Islands separates the Atlantic from the Indian Ocean. The Atlantic includes all adjacent semienclosed seas that connect with it.

Atmosphere

The gaseous (air) envelope that surrounds the earth. The weight exerted by the atmosphere at sea level is 14.7 pounds per square inch.

Atoll

A ringline "coral" island or group of islands encircling or nearly encircling a lagoon.

Barnacle

Any one of the various members of the crustacean family. One type *(Lepas)* attaches itself to the hulls of ships, whereas the acorn barnacle *(Balanus)* covers both coastal rocks and ships' bottoms.

Basin

A depression of the ocean floor, more or less equidimensional in form and extent.

Bathymetry

The measurement of depths of water in the oceans to determine bottom contours.

Bathyscaphe

An untethered submarine vehicle, invented by Auguste Picard. In principle, bathyscaphes consist of a pressure-resistant ball hull hanging from a huge metal envelope filled with a lifting fluid. In 1954, a French bathyscaphe reached a 13,287-foot depth.

Bathythermograph

A device for obtaining the ocean water's temperature at various depths.

Bends

A diving hazard, also called Caisson sickness, caused by sudden decompression, when bubbles of nitrogen and other related gases are released into the body tissue. It may be fatal or permanently disabling and can be prevented by means of staged ascents to the surface.

Benthic

Pertaining to that portion of the marine environment inhabited by marine organisms that live permanently in or on the bottom, or all submarine bottom terrain, regardless of water depth.

Bioluminescence

The production of light by living organisms as a result of a chemical reaction inside their cells or organs, or outside in the form of a secretion.

Biosphere

The sum total of all living things inhabiting the earth and its atmosphere.

Bivalve

Aquatic animals, such as clams, oysters, and scallops, having a shell composed of two distinct parts.

British thermal unit (Btu)

The amount of heat required to raise the temperature of 1 pound of water 1°F under stated conditions of temperature and pressure. The Btu is the standard unit for measuring the quantity of heat energy.

Cephalopods

Marine mollusks, including squids, octopuses, and Nautilus.

Continental rise

That part of the continental margin between the continental slope and the abyssal plain, except in oceanic trenches.

Continental shelf

The part of the continental margin between the shore and the continental slope.

Continental slope

The surface sloping seaward from a shelf edge into greater depths. The sloping part of the continental margin between the continental shelf and the continental rise.

Coral

Biology: Marine coelenterates, solitary or colonial, that form a hard external covering of calcium compounds or other materials. The corals that form large reefs are limited to warm, shallow waters, whereas those forming solitary, minute growths may be found in colder waters, to great depths.

Geology: The concretion of coral polyp shells, composed almost wholly of calcium carbonate, forming reefs and treelike and globular masses. May also include calcareous algae and other organisms producing calcareous secretions, such as bryozoans and hydrozoans.

Core

A cylindrical sample of soil, ice, snow, or rock obtained by a hollow tube (corer) driven into the material. The removed sample is used for scientific analysis.

Corrosion

A chemical attack on a metallic surface, generally causing a structural weakening or erosion of the metal.

Crustaceans

Jointed animals (mainly aquatic) with hard external shells, including crabs, shrimp, lobsters, crayfish, and barnacles.

Current

In general, a horizontal movement of water. Currents are classified as tidal and nontidal. Tidal currents are caused by gravitational interactions among the sun, moon, and earth. They are a part of the same general movement of the sea that is manifested in its rise and fall, called a tide. Nontidal currents include the permanent currents in the ocean's general circulatory systems as well as temporary currents caused by meteorological variability.

Deep scattering layers

The region or strata in the ocean that scatter or return vertically directed sound, as in depth sounding. These layers are located at depths of about 900 to 1200 feet during the day and at or near the surface at night. The layers are evidently of biological origin.

Detritus

Particulate matter resulting from the degeneration and decay of organisms or inorganic substances in nature.

Diatoms

Microscopic algae with an external skeleton of silica.

Dinoflagellates

Minute, one-celled animals (protozoans), most of which are not visible to the naked eye. They occur universally in the oceans' surface layers. Several genera of protozoans are capable of producing bioluminescence.

Diurnal

Active by day; having a daily cycle; recurrent each day. A semidurnal has a period or cycle of approximately half a lunar day (12.42 solar hours), and tides and tidal currents are said to be semidiurnal when two flood and two ebb periods occur on each lunar day.

Dorsal

Referring to the upper side, such as the dorsal fin; the opposite of ventral.

Ebb currents

Currents associated with a decrease in the height of a tide. Ebb currents generally flow seaward.

El Niño

Spanish for the Christ Child. A warm ocean current that appears about every 10 years at Christmas time, flowing southward along the Peruvian coast. It is responsible for disastrous kills of fish and sea birds and extremely heavy rains on the land.

Estuary

A bay, such as at the mouth of a river, where the river water mixes with and measurably dilutes ocean water.

Fauna

The animal life characteristic of a particular environment or region.

Filter feeders
Animals that feed on minute organisms suspended in the water, by using a screening and capturing (filtering) mechanism.

Flood currents
Currents associated with an increase in the height of a tide, generally setting in the same direction as the tidal progression and perpendicular to the cotidal lines (lines on a map passing through all points at which high waters occur at the same time).

Freshwater
Water containing fewer than 1000 parts of dissolved salts per million parts of water.

Geophysics
The study of the earth by quantitative physical methods, such as thermal, gravity, magnetic, electric, and seismic techniques.

Gulf Stream
A North Atlantic Ocean current running northeastward off the east coast of the United States. A segment of the Gulf Stream system, the Gulf Stream extends from the region off Cape Hatteras to an area southeast of the Grand Banks. It continues the flow of the Florida current to the North Atlantic current. Part of the oceans' general, surface circulation.

Guyot
A flat-topped submarine mountain.

Hurricanes
Storms that start over water (as do typhoons) and consist of winds rotating counterclockwise at velocities of 75 to 100 mph. They develop in low pressure areas and are usually accompanied by very high tides. Their diameters may range from 150 to 300 miles.

Hydrostatic pressure

The pressure at a given depth based on the water mass above that depth. Usually measured in pounds per square inch.

Invertebrates

Animals lacking a backbone and an internal skeleton.

Larvae

Free-living, immature forms that have developed from a fertilized egg but must undergo a series of size and shape changes before assuming the characteristic features of the adult organism.

Magnetic anomaly

The difference between the intensity of the magnetic field at a point and the theoretically calculated value. Anomalies are interpreted in regard to the depth, size, shape, and magnetization of the geological features causing them.

Magnetometer

An instrument used to measure the magnetic force of the ocean bottom and miscellaneous underwater magnetic information.

Mammals

"Warm-blooded" (that is, capable of maintaining a stable body temperature by physiological means) vertebrates having mammary glands and body hair. Other distinguishing characteristics are red blood corpuscles, three middle ear bones, a diaphragm separating the thorax from the abdomen, sebaceous and sweat glands in the skin, and usually an external ear or pinna protruding from the side of the head.

Mean sea level

The mean surface level determined by averaging all stages of the tide over a 19-year period.

Mesozoic era
The interval of geological time from about 230 million to 70 million years ago. Also known as the Age of Reptiles.

Metamorphic rocks
Rocks that have metamorphized, or changed, after being subjected to changes in pressure, temperature, and chemical environment.

Mollusk
A division of the animal kingdom containing clams, mussels, oysters, snails, octopuses, and squids. They are characterized by an organ that secretes a shell.

Mud
Pelagic or terrigenous detrital material consisting of particles smaller than sand, such as an undifferentiated sediment made up of particles mostly within the silt–clay range smaller than 0.0025 inch (0.0625 millimeter).

Nansen bottle
An oceanographic water-sampling bottle made of a metal alloy that reacts little seawater and is equipped with a rotary valve at each end so that when it is rotated at depth, the valves close and lock shut, entrapping a water sample and setting the reversing thermometers. This bottle is named for its designer, Fridtjof Nansen.

Nautical mile
A unit of distance designed to equal about 1 minute of arc of latitude. Its length is 6080.20 feet, approximately 1.15 times as long as the statute mile of 5280 feet.

Nontidal currents
Currents caused by forces other than tidal forces. The Gulf Stream, Japan, Labrador, and equatorial currents are part of the general ocean circulation and are classed as nontidals. Also in this category are river discharges and temporary currents set up by winds.

North Atlantic current
A North Atlantic Ocean current running northeastward from southeast of the Grand Banks to the British Isles. Part of the general surface circulation of the oceans, the North Atlantic current continues the flow of the Gulf Stream to the Norwegian and Canary currents.

North equatorial currents
Currents setting westward in the North Atlantic and North Pacific oceans and in the Indian Ocean from about October to July. Part of the oceans' general, surface circulation.

Pacific Ocean
The ocean area (63.8 million square miles) bounded on the east by the continents of the Americas, on the north by the Bering Strait, on the west by a line from the Malay Peninsula through Cape Londonderry in Australia and Tasmania, then along meridian 147°E to Antarctica. The Pacific includes all adjacent semienclosed seas that connect with it.

Pelagic division
A primary division of the ocean that includes the entire mass of water. It is made up of the Neritic Province, the water shallower than 200 meters (660 feet), and the Oceanic Province, water deeper than 200 meters.

Peru current
A South Pacific Ocean current flowing northward along the west coast of Latin America. Part of the general, surface circulation of the ocean. Often called the Humboldt current after the German scientist, Alexander von Humboldt, who first recorded its temperature in 1802.

pH
A measure of acidity and alkalinity; A pH of 7 represents neutrality; a pH of below 7, acidity; a pH above 7, alkalinity.

Photosynthesis
The process that produces plant tissue in green plants. The process requires sunlight, carbon dioxide, water, and chlorophyll (the green coloring matter in plants). One of the basic support systems for life on earth, photosynthesis returns oxygen to the atmosphere and removes carbon dioxide. Animals use the oxygen and give up carbon dioxide as a waste product.

Phytoplankton
The plant forms of plankton, including dinoflagellates and diatoms.

Plankton
Passively floating or weakly motile aquatic plants and animals.

Portuguese man-of-war
Scientific name, *Physalia*, the Portuguese man-of-war is a large coelenterate (of the class Hydrozoa), consisting of a colony of polyps. It drifts on the ocean's surface buoyed by a gas-filled float. Its long tentacles may hang down as much as 100 feet. These tentacles are equipped with powerful stinging cells (nematocysts) that can be very dangerous to humans.

Pycnocline
A vertical gradient in the ocean where its density changes rapidly.

Radar
From "radio detection and ranging." Basically, a system or technique of using beamed reflected and time radiowaves to detect, locate or track objects.

Radioisotope
The radioactive form of an element; may occur naturally or be artificially produced, as by neutron bombardment of a stable (non-radioactive) element.

Remote sensing
The collection of information about an object by a recording device that is not in physical contact with it.

Rip current
A strong current of limited area flowing outward from the shore. It is characterized as a region of agitated water in which the regular wave pattern is interrupted. Rip currents are caused by the escape of water, by means of waves, between a shore and an offshore bank, shoal, or reef. The rush of the escaping water is accentuated by its flow through a gap in the reef.

Saline water
Any water containing more than 1000 parts per million of dissolved salts.

Saturation diving
A diving method whereby the human body is allowed to reach a condition of complete saturation with dissolved gases at the pressures encountered in a given working depth.

Scuba
Self-contained, underwater breathing apparatus. Any free-diving unit containing the elements necessary to support life underwater.

Seamount
A seafloor mountain generally formed as a submarine volcano.

Sea urchin
An echinoderm (class Echinoidea) that possesses a thin spiny shell (either spherical or flattened) and suckerlike tube feet. The familiar sand dollar is a type of sea urchin.

Seawater
Water containing approximately 35,000 parts per million of dissolved salts.

Sedimentary rocks
Rocks formed from accumulated sediments derived from disintegrated rock fragments or dissolved minerals precipitated from solution or the remains of animals and plants.

Shipworm
A marine wormlike clam that burrows in submerged wood, such as wharves or wooden ships.

Skin diving
Diving without the use of scuba.

Sonar
Acronym derived from "sound navigation and ranging." The method of equipment used for determining, by means of underwater sound techniques, the presence, location, and nature of objects in the ocean. Passive sonar is a listening technique or device. In active sonar, various types of sound frequencies are sent out to bounce off a submerged target and return as an echo.

Sound velocimeter
A device to measure directly the speed of sound in seawater.

Species
A specific type of plant or animal.

Stratigraphy
The study of the order of rock strata, their age and structure, and their distribution and composition.

Substrate
The substance on or in which an organism lives and grows.

Subtropical convergence
A region of convergent currents marked by a rapid increase in

surface-water density toward the poles. Water sinking farther from the equator is denser and so will sink to a greater depth.

Surf (or surf zone)

Waves breaking on a shore (or the areas near the shore where waves break).

Swell

A large, more-or-less smooth wave.

Symbiosis

The relationship between organisms of two species that is essential to the survival of one or both members of the partnership.

Synoptic

Referring to observations made simultaneously over a wide area, such as the physical properties of the atmosphere and weather.

Syzygy

The position of the moon when it is full or new. The two opposite points in the moon's orbit at which it is in conjunction with or opposition to the sun.

Taxonomy

The classification of organisms into groups reflecting their similarity and differences (kingdom, phylum, class, order, family, genus, and species).

Tectonics

The study of the origin and development of the earth's structural features.

Teredo

Shipworms of the two-shelled (bivalve) genus of the family Teredinidae. These mollusks have shells that can cut into wood.

These animals attach themselves to wood on pilings and boats and eat the wood, digesting the cellulose.

Thermocline
A gradient in the ocean in which the temperature changes rapidly.

Thermodynamics
The study of energy conversions and exchanges. A thermodynamic system is one in which the energy properties are considered. The first law of thermodynamics states that the total energy in the system remains constant; the second law states that the degree of randomness (entropy) in the system tends to increase.

Tidal current
A horizontal movement of the water caused by gravitational inter-actions among the sun, moon, and earth.

Tide
The periodic rise and fall of the ocean water resulting from gravita-tional interactions among the sun, moon, and earth.

Transducer
A device that converts one form of energy into another, such as electrical to acoustic, or vice versa.

Trench
A long, narrow and deep depression of the ocean floor that has relatively steep sides.

Turbulence
A state of fluid flow in which the instantaneous velocities exhibit irregular and apparently random fluctuations.

Zooplankton
Animal forms of plankton.

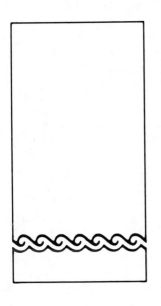

BIBLIOGRAPHY

Ballard, R. D. "How We Found the *Titanic.*" *National Geographic* 168 (1985).

Beer, T. *Environmental Oceanography: An Introduction to the Behavior of Coastal Waters:* Oxford, England: Pergamon Press, 1983.

Behrman, D. *The New World of the Oceans, Men and Oceanography.* Boston: Little, Brown, 1969.

Berger, A. L. ed. *Climatic Variations and Variability: Facts and Theories:* Hingham, Mass.: Kluwer Boston, 1981.

Briscoe, Melbourne G. "A Primer on the U.S. Contribution to the World Ocean Circulation Experimentation," College Station, Tex.: U.S. Planning Office for WOCE, U.S WOCE Planning Report No. 4, 1986.

Broecker, W. S. *Chemical Oceanography.* New York: Harcourt Brace Jovanovich, 1974.

Burton, Maurice, and Burton, Robert. *Encyclopedia of Fish.* Hong Kong: Mandarin Publishers, 1975.

Carson, R. L. *The Sea Around Us,* rev. ed. New York: Oxford University Press, 1961.

Committee on Marine Structures. *Recommendations of the Intra-agency Ship Structure Committee's Fiscal 1988 Research Program.* Washington, D.C.: National Academy Press, 1987.

Congressional Workshop on Advanced Materials Research and Development. *Report to the Committee on Science and Technology.* U.S. House of Representatives, Ninety-Ninth Congress. Washington, D.C.: U.S. Government Printing Office, June 1985.

Cushing, D. H. *Climate and Fisheries.* London: Academic Press, 1982.

Cutshall, N. H. "A Chemist's View of Oceanography." *Journal of Chemical Education* 54(3) (1977).

Duursma, E. K., and Dawson, R., eds. *Marine Organic Chemistry: Evolution, Composition, Interactions and Chemistry of Organic Matter in Seawater.* New York: Elsevier, 1981.

Emiliani, C. *The Oceanic Lithosphere.* New York: Wiley Interscience, 1981.

Future Ocean Research, Scientific Committee for Ocean Research (SCOR) for the Intergovernmental Oceanographic Commission, Halifax, 1982.

Gilbert, Perry W. *Sharks and Survival.* Boston: Heath, 1963.

Glantz, M. H., and J. D. Thompson eds. *Resource Management and Environmental Uncertainty: Lessons from Coastal Upwelling Fisheries.* New York: John Wiley & Sons, 1982.

Gower, J. R., ed. *Oceanography from Space.* New York: Plenum, 1981.

Gross, M. G. *Oceanography: A View of the Earth,* 3rd ed. Englewood Cliffs, N.J.: Prentice–Hall, 1982.

Groves, D. G. "Materials, Society and the World's Oceans." *Materials and Society Journal* 11(4) (1987): New York: Pergammon Press, 1987.

Groves, D. G., and Hunt, L. M. *The Ocean World Encyclopedia.* New York: McGraw–Hill, 1980.

Halstead, Bruce W. *Dangerous Marine Animals.* Cambridge, Md.: Cornell Maritime Press, 1959.

Herald, Earl S. *Living Fishes of the World.* Garden City, N.Y.: Doubleday, 1961.

Hunt, L. M., and Groves, D. G. *A Glossary of Ocean Science and Undersea Technology Terms.* Arlington, Va.: Compass Publications, 1965.

Idyll, C. P., ed. *Exploring the Ocean World, a History of Oceanography.* New York: T. Y. Crowell, 1969.

Ingram, C. J. "High Resolution Side Scan Sonar/Subbottom Profiling to 6,000 Mile Water Depth." Paper presented at the Pacific Congress on Marine Technology, Hawaii, 1986.

Intergovernmental Oceanographic Commission. *Integrated Global Ocean Stations System (IGOSS), General Plan and Implementation Programme 1977–1982.* Paris: UNESCO Marine Information Centre, 1972.

Intergovernmental Oceanographic Commission. *Oceanographic Products and Methods of Analysis and Prediction.* Paris: UNESCO Marine Information Centre, 1977.

Johnson, A. S., ed. *Research Requirements in Support of Continental Scientific Drilling.* Washington, D.C.: Deep Observation and Sampling of the Earth's Continental Crust, 1986.

Levington, J. S. *Marine Ecology.* Englewood Cliffs, N.J.: Prentice–Hall, 1982.

McKelvey, V. E. "Subsea Mineral Resources." *U.S. Geological Survey Bulletin* (1986).

Meltzer, David J., et al., eds. *American Archaeology Past and Future.* Washington, D.C.: Smithsonian Institution Press, 1986.

Muir, W. "Early Sailing Ship Archaeology and Reconstruction." *Journal Astrolabe* 2(1) Key West, Florida. (1985).

National Academy of Engineering. *Toward Fulfillment of a National Ocean Commitment.* Washington, D.C.: National Academy of Sciences, 1972.

National Academy of Sciences. *An Assessment of Computational Resources Required for Ocean Circulation Modelling.* Washington, D.C.: National Academy Press, 1982.

National Academy of Sciences. *Biological Oceanography.* Washington, D.C.: National Academy of Sciences, 1975.

National Academy of Sciences. *Continental Scientific Drilling Program.* Washington, D.C.: National Academy of Sciences, 1979.

National Academy of Sciences. *The Continuing Quest.* Washington, D.C.: National Academy of Sciences, 1979.

National Academy of Sciences. *Geodynamics in the 1980's.* Washington, D.C.: National Academy of Sciences, 1980.

National Academy of Sciences. *Global Ocean Flux Study.* Washington, D.C.: National Academy Press, 1984.

National Academy of Sciences. *Marine Chemistry.* Washington, D.C.: National Academy of Sciences, 1971.

National Academy of Sciences. *Opportunities in Chemistry.* Washington, D.C.: National Academy Press, 1985.

National Academy of Sciences. *Opportunities for Research in the Geological Sciences.* Washington, D.C.: National Academy of Sciences, 1983.

National Academy of Sciences. *Orientations in Geochemistry.* Washington, D.C.: National Academy of Sciences, 1973.

National Academy of Sciences. *Recommendations for the Interagency Ship Structure Committee's Fiscal 1988 Research Program.* Washington, D.C.: National Academy Press, 1987.

National Academy of Sciences. *Science and Technology—A Five Year Outlook.* Washington, D.C.: National Academy of Sciences, 1979.

National Academy of Sciences. *Strengthening Research and Innovation in the Martime Industries.* Washington, D.C.: National Academy Press, 1986.

National Environmental Satellite, Data, and Information Service. *Nature's Scorekeepers.* Washington, D.C.: U.S. Government Printing Office, Report #S/N003-017-00521-6, 1985.

National Oceanic and Atmospheric Administration. *The NOAA Diving Manual—Diving or Science and Technology.* Washington, D.C.: U.S. Government Printing Office, 1975.

National Science Foundation. *Earth Science Research and NSF.* Washington, D.C.: National Science Foundation, Report NSF85-26, 1985.

Nybakken, J. W. *Marine Biology: An Ecological Approach.* New York: Harper & Row, 1982.

Ocean Affairs Board. *Biological Oceanography.* Washington, D.C.: National Academy of Sciences, 1975.

Office of Technology Assessment. *Exploring Our New Ocean Frontier.* Washington, D.C.: U.S. Government Printing Office, Publication #OTA-0-343, 1987.

Office of Technology Assessment. *Marine Minerals: Exploring Our New Ocean Frontier.* Washington, D.C.: U.S. Government Printing Office, OTA Report 0-343, 1987.

Office of Technology Assessment. *Technology and Oceanography.* Washington, D.C.: U.S. Government Printing Office, 1987.

Parsons, T. R., Takahaski, M., and Hargrove, B. *Biological Oceanographic Processes.* Elmsford, N.Y.: Pergamon Press, 1977.

Perry, R. H., and Green D., eds. *Perry's Chemical Engineer's Handbook*, 6th ed. New York: McGraw–Hill, 1984.

Pickard, G. L., and Emery, W. J., eds. *Descriptive Physical Oceanography: An Introduction*, 4th ed. Elmsford, N.Y.: Pergamon Press, 1982.

Pickard, G. L., and Pond, S., eds. *Introductory Dynamic Oceanography.* Elmsford, N.Y.: Pergamon Press, 1978.

Riehl, H. *Climate and Weather in the Tropics.* New York: Academic Press, 1979.

Ross, D. A. *Introduction to Oceanography,* Englewood Cliffs, N.J.: Prentice–Hall, 1982.

Ryan, P.R. "The *Titanic* Revisited (1986)." *Oceanus* 28 (4) (1986): Woods Hole Oceanographic Institution.

Scheur, P. J., ed. *Marine Natural Products: Chemical and Biological Perspectives,* vol. 3. New York: Academic Press, 1980.

Shepard, F. P. *Submarine Geology,* 3rd ed. New York: Harper & Row, 1973.

Stowe, K. *Essentials of Ocean Sciences.* New York: John Wiley & Sons, 1987.

Technologies for Prehistoric and Historic Preservation. Washington, D.C.: Office of Technology Assessment, 1987.

Technologies for Underwater Archaeology and Maritime Preservation. Washington, D.C.: Office of Technology Assessment, 1987.

Throckmorton, P. "Marine Archaeology." *Oceanus* 28(1) (1985): Woods Hole Oceanographic Institution.

U.S. Department of Energy. *Ecological Research Division Marine Research Program.* Washington, D.C.: U.S. Department of Energy, 1983.

Von Arx, W. S. *An Introduction to Physical Oceanography.* Reading, Mass.: Addison–Wesley, 1962.

Ward, Ritchie. *Into the Ocean World, the Biology of the Sea.* New York: Knopf, 1974.

Wood, F. G. *Marine Mammals and Man: The Navy's Porpoises and Sea Lions.* Washington, D.C.: R. B. Luce, 1973.

————. *The NOAA Diving Manual.* Washington, D.C.: U.S. Department of Commerce, 1979.

World Meteorological Organization. "The GARP Atlantic Tropical Experiment (GATE) Monograph." Global Atmospheric Research Program (GARP) Publication Series No. 25. Geneva, Switzerland: WMO, 1982.

————. "The Physical Basis of Climate and Climate Modelling, Report of the International Study Conference in Stockholm, 29 July–10 August 1974." Global Atmospheric Research Program (GARP) Publication Series No. 16. New York: UNIPUB, and Geneva, Switzerland; WMO, 1975.

World Meteorological Organization/Intergovernmental Oceanographic Commission/International Council of Scientific Unions/World Climate Program. Papers presented at the meeting in Tokyo, May 1981. Available from UNIPUB, New York, N.Y. and WMO, Geneva, Switzerland.

Worsley, Thomas R., Nance, R. Damian, and Moody, Judith B. "Tectonic Cyles and the History of the Earth's Biochemical and Paleoceanographic Records." *Paleoceanography* 1(3) (1986): 233–263.

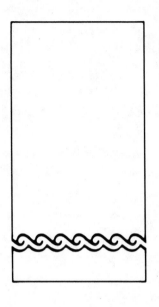

INDEX

191